THE OCCULT
an Introduction

Gareth Knight

The Occult:

an Introduction

Kahn & Averill, London

This completely revised edition, published in 1990 by
Kahn & Averill
9 Harrington Road, London SW7 3ES

First edition published in 1975
Second edition published in 1990.

British Library Cataloguing in Publication Data

Knight, Gareth
    The occult : an introduction. – 2nd ed.
    1. Paranormal phenomena
    I. Title
    133

ISBN 1–871082–09–9

Typeset in Galliard 10/12 point by
Mathematical Composition Setters Ltd, Ivy Street, Salisbury

Printed in Great Britain by
Halstan & Co Ltd., Amersham, Bucks

CONTENTS

PART ONE
The Golden Thread of Occult Tradition

1 FACT OR FICTION?

An overview of the occult

It is not easy to make a rational approach to the occult. This is because it is neither an easy nor an entirely rational subject, and it also covers a large and diverse field.

Its sheer size makes a short study of it as difficult as a short study of 'science' or of 'religion'. In fact it is basically a study of both, of 'science' *and* 'religion', though not science and religion in their ordinary sense. Occultism is very largely the study of *rejected* science and religion.

Now why should we study a subject that has been rejected in the course of time by the accepted establishment of learning? There are in fact good reasons for this, and not all concerned with the academic pursuit of useless or outworn knowledge. The question is whether the subject-matter of occultism has been rejected for the right reasons!

The 'world view' of any civilisation changes as it progresses in time and at any particular stage certain beliefs may seem to be disproved, or to be of little practical import and so not merit further investigation. For instance, what science has rejected as a false world view of the heavens astronomically, may yet be an important line of study of the inner structure of the soul of man, projected forth from his own psyche in speculation about the unknown.

Similarly, what may have been rejected as heretical or impious by religious authority may in fact be an important area, not of religion but of science. For instance was Renaissance magic a psychological therapy before its time, rather than a superstitious throwback to ancient times?

Other areas of the occult may quite deservedly have been rejected from scientific or religious established thinking, and yet thrive in the popular consciousness. There must even here be a reason for such beliefs to continue, be they so apparently trivial as belief in bad luck through breaking a mirror or spilling salt. Some apparent chimera of fancy strikes a chord of recognition deep in the human heart. The occult researcher does not dismiss such things out of hand. He pursues them sympathetically.

There is, of course, a largely subjective element in all such studies. And indeed another definition of the occult might well be the study of the subjective as if it were objective. Or alternatively a study of the objective as if it were subjective.

An example of the kind of difficulty we face can be culled from the short novel of Henry James entitled *The Turn of the Screw*.

On the face of it this most spine-chilling of ghost stories, (which unlike many literary attempts in this genre, is completely 'authentic' as far as its description of paranormal phenomena go), tells the story of a young lady who is appointed to be governess of two children at a deserted mansion, in the company only of an illiterate housekeeper. Whilst there she begins to discover, to her horror, a subtle and curiously adult perversity in her two young charges, and then to be aware of two physically observable 'horrors' about the place.

One is the 'presence' of a former gardener, Peter Quint, and the other the former governess of the children. It transpires that Quint, a creature of low morals and appetites, has been killed in suspicious circumstances, probably by persons who had good cause to hate him, and the governess, Miss Jessel, who was his lover, has committed suicide.

The horrifying realisation that gradually breaks in upon the governess is that these two creatures are 'earthbound' spirits, hanging about the place, striving to possess the souls and bodies of the two young children, a boy and a girl, so that they can continue their illicit love through them in a bizarre and incestuous relationship. Events, such as the otherwise innocent boy being expelled from school, seem to point towards the certainty of all this and eventually, in desperation, the governess tries to extort confessions of guilt and remorse from the children in an attempt to exorcise the evil influence. In the climax of this the boy dies of shock.

It is not exactly a pleasant story when conceived as a ghost story, but it takes on more disturbing meanings if viewed from other perspectives. Suppose, for example, we do not take the governess's diagnosis of the situation at face value? Suppose Peter Quint and Miss Jessel are not ghosts but her own hallucinations? Suppose it is *she* who is sick – at first projecting a totally unlikely innocence upon her young charges, and then endowing them with the evil of her own repressed sexual fantasies? Is any apparently secretive and conspiratorial behaviour in the children all her own imagination? Or, yet worse, is it the natural behaviour of two children who find themselves under the control of a neurotic and increasingly morbid woman? Are we in fact seeing insanity through the eyes of the insane?

There is not space to pursue this line of enquiry here, and yet more interpretations may be put upon the story. But it serves as an illustration of the difficulties we are faced with in an investigation of the occult – at any level. We can never be entirely sure of the validity of the facts we are dealing with – or their proper perspective – because of the shifting boundary of the subjective and objective as we try to push knowledge and experience beyond the fairly well-defined categories of the physical world.

Many approaches to the occult are indeed more fictional than real. The easy target of the unbalanced psychic has been well portrayed by Noel Coward in Madame Arcarty in *Blithe Spirit*. And there is also a field of fiction relating to the occult as there is, in science-fiction, a field of fiction relating to science.

In both genres some stories are more 'authentic' than others. The fault of most occult fiction is that in their search for fictional effectiveness the authors portray psychic and interior sensations as if they were physical. This, in fact, is bad craftsmanship as well as a misrepresentation of the facts. The horrors of a psychical obsession, for example, a crumbling of the structures of personality, is more terrifying than the physical apperception of clanking chains and hollow groans.

Again, the fictional tends to concentrate upon the sensational and the perverse. Obsession, which we have already been pressed into mentioning twice, is a rare pathology. There is, in fact, much spiritual good and psychological health to be found in the proper study of the occult.

Unfortunately the sensational and the perverse make the best headlines and sell the most paperbacks. And one cannot fail to censure the type of popular novelist who profitably writes it all up from a sensational angle and then utters portentous moral warnings about its dangers. Such a dual approach is almost certain to attract the morbid curiosity of the immature and unbalanced toward the worst elements of the subject. There are indeed certain traditional attitudes in both evangelical and catholic churches that condemn the whole subject out of hand on theological grounds. This is a pity for in occultism there are insights into the structure of the human psyche that strengthen and confirm the traditional standpoint of certain areas of mystical theology. There is an opportunity for dialogue by a number of disciplines that have not communicated one with another before.

If psychiatrists, theologians, and occultists could meet together on common ground, the resultant insights might well have repercussions far beyond these disciplines, into attitudes toward the world about us; new attitudes to mankind's responsibilities to itself and the planet upon which we live.

It is not too bizarre to affirm that perhaps explosion of an atomic bomb might have effects on the psychological and inner structure of the planet, as well as on the constituents of its physical husk. This would have sounded fantastic a few years ago. To some it may still do so. But to those who have the kind of synthesising mind such as that of Teilhard de Chardin, it may not appear so strange. Teilhard was a scientist, mystic and theologian, looking at things anew. There is yet more to discover from the non-physical and intellectually rejected.

This is what we intend to investigate in this book. The all embracing nature of the subject makes it difficult to find a starting point. Therefore our treatment is threefold. First, a discursive look at some of the main strands and features of the subject; then an alphabetical glossary of a number of specialist topics within it; and finally some practical exercises to help get you started.

2 FUNCTIONS, ELEMENTS & ARCHETYPES
A psychology of the occult

The psychologist C.G. Jung has come closest to confirming some of the traditional occult views – although most Jungian analysts would hesitate to be bracketed with the occult. Similarly most occult teachers would be reluctant to explain all their beliefs or experiences in the light of analytical psychology. But there *is* common ground, because Jung sees man as having links with all other humans and other forms of consciousness.

Jung posits a personal unconscious and a collective unconscious which can be expressed diagramatically as a kind of sub-marine mountain range. The islands are our individual conscious identities but there is an individual unconsciousness under the surface, and deeper down in the pyschic strata a common unconsciousness which has a life of its own and in which we all participate. The collective unconscious also has its layers giving an unconscious linkage between members of one family, tribe, nation, species.

individual conscious identities

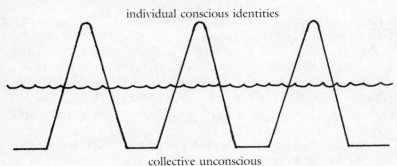

collective unconscious

With the unconscious, being by definition unconscious, we are at
something of a disadvantage – for how can we be conscious of it?
Jung thinks it makes itself evident by various kinds of upwellings into
consciousness – images, emotions, attitudes, prejudices and so on.

Here there is some difference from the Freudian point of view
which tends to see the *sub*conscious (the term Freud preferred), as
the repository for repressed desires and taboos – particularly of a
sexual nature.

Jung however takes a more positive view in saying that the personal
unconscious is not merely a dustbin of rejected consciousness, but
has a deep and wise concern for us. Thus his approach to psychological problems is not so much one of analysis in the Freudian sense –
with a view to regurgitating unacceptable experiences or attitudes –
but one of integration. That is, taking into consciousness those parts
of the unconscious which will make for a more balanced human
being.

This view of the role of the unconscious almost as a separate
identity, poses some profound questions with regard to other
disciplines. For it can verge on religion in the case of those who feel
they are guided by a personal God. It can also be applied to primitive
ancestor-worship or to spiritualist communication with the
departed.

The unconscious has also entered the field of ancient science, for
when man faces the unknown he projects images and theories into it,
which are – according to Jung – a reflection of the structure of man's
own psyche.

Thus we find a marked similarity between various ancient beliefs on
the structure of the universe, and the 'gods' or forces that make it
work. There is a tendency for the numbers 3, 4, 7 and 12 to crop up
in such cosmologies.

Jung pays particular attention to the number 4 – the quarternio.
For this figures much in early theories of the structure of the universe
– the belief that there were four elements (Earth, Air, Fire and
Water) from various mixtures of which all things are made. This is
reflected in the principal states of matter; solid, liquid, gaseous and
radiation or heat. But it was also applied to the psychic constitution
of man – there being phlegmatic earthy types or emotional watery
types, and so on.

Jung has in fact suggested a modern version of this by formulating
four psychological types. In place of Earth, Water, Air and Fire he

posits Sensation, Feeling, Intuition and Intellect. All of us form one
or other of these psychological types, though the pure type is rare.
Not only this, there appears to be a certain relation between the four
functions. Feeling is diametrically opposed to Thinking; Sensation
diametrically opposed to Intuition. And of the four functions, half
will be conscious and half unconscious. We each partake of all four
but we consciously express only one in full, with two of them to a
greater or lesser extent unconscious and one fully unconscious. This
is best expressed in a diagram of the psyche being like a ball floating in
water.

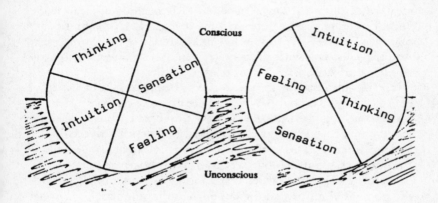

The thinking type tends to try to solve everything by a rational
approach and thus may appear rather cold and arid, but is subject to
occasional up-rushes of uncontrolled feeling.

The feeling type, the polar opposite, assesses things in a feeling
way; this is the patriot, the backbone of any society, club, family or
nation. Here it is thinking that is repressed, so strange and wild
theories may be formulated as a justification for emotional loyalties
held.

The sensation type is down-to-earth and practical but liable to
uncontrolled up-rushes of woolly idealism or religious enthusiasms.

On the other hand the intuitional type has a facility for living life
successfully on hunches but may be subject to strong impulses of
sensuality.

This is just the bare bones of the matter. The interested reader can
fill in his own assessment of the combination of types.

Another factor is that of the archetypes. These are not easy to describe and tend to have a different role according to the sex of each person. They are ways in which the unconscious part of the psyche expresses itself either through dream, fantasy or projection. One might call them filters or lenses for the unconscious.

Of major importance are the archetypes of the *animus* and *anima* sometimes called the *contrasexual image*.

The *anima* in man consists of all ideas of the female – not only personal but inherited via the unconscious, and is most readily discernible when it is being projected onto a flesh and blood woman. In this we have the situation of the woman being romantically idealised, being 'put on a pedestal'. All manner of near-divine qualities are projected onto her by the lover, although to any objective observer she may be no more attractive than a hat rack. And this in effect is what she is – a convenient peg on which to hang an *anima* projection.

It is possible not only for the *anima* to be projected but also for a man to be possessed by it – which is perhaps more commonplace and less far-reaching in its possible effects. An impatient lover becomes moody, upset, touchy – possessed of all the negative aspects of the 'eternal woman'. This is the basis for the traditional 'lovers tiff' – amusing to the outsider but very painful to the participants.

There are other archetypes that Jung focuses attention upon for the purpose of his psycho-therapy such as the animus; the persona; the shadow; the wise old man; the miraculous child.

Briefly, the *animus* is the contra-sexual image in woman. It tends to be more like a shadowy *group* of male advisers. When an animus possession is running it manifests as bossy arbitrary statements thus perpetuating the traditional idea of 'female logic'.

The *persona* is common to all of us and is not so much an archetype in the sense of the others. It is the mask we all assume in our relationships with other people. William Blake seems to be the only person of whom it is recorded that "he never wore a mask" but had the simplicity and integrity to present his soul naked to the world.

The *shadow* is a nasty character, being all the things we most detest in ourselves. It can have an ugly face when projected upon other people, either individually or collectively. This results in the individual 'bête noire', the person we gratuitously detest, or it can be projected onto a whole group, producing racial prejudice or xenophobia. It is something of an educative experience to realise that the unlovely qualities we project upon others are in fact characteristics of our own selves that we find difficult to accept.

The *wise old man* in relation to the occult, we shall return to again, in the concept of 'masters' or 'gurus', whilst the *miraculous child* is an important religious archetype. Our excursion into analytical psychology has been necessitated by the fact that there is common ground between mystical theology, analytical psychology and occultism, and each one is difficult to explain without reference to the others.

For the moment we shall simply note that the *wise old man* archetype is a reputed source of great and arcane wisdom, and the *miraculous child* a source of great wonder and 'new life'. At their more superficial levels they show in the great respect for age in certain societies and in sentimentality over the young in others.

However, it is not our purpose to do more than outline the Jungian psychological scheme of things. Our interest lies more in extensions upon them that take us far beyond the psychological consulting-room.

3   OLD GODS AND STARRY SYMBOLS
A ground-plan of the occult

The beliefs of antiquity that mainly concern us are the cults of the pagan gods. They are of more than antiquarian interest, and are in fact very much alive and kicking all about us. Some of them may be recognised in the Jungian archetypes. The anima, or femme fatale, has close connections with the Greek goddess Aphrodite, or the Roman Venus, she who rose from the sea of the unconscious depths.

But there are many other ancient gods. We find that they represent characteristics of the human soul projected onto the universe, and particularly into the heavens, in the panorama of the sun, moon and planets performing their wandering movements before the backdrop of the fixed stars.

Thus we have, common to almost all mankind, the ten-fold schema of Earth, Moon, Mercury, Venus, Sun, Mars, Jupiter, Saturn, Fixed Stars, Prime Movement.

The Earth is associated with the Great Mother, Mother Nature, she who brings forth all organic life as we know it. It is also the Sphere of the Elements, which as Fire, Earth, Air and Water correspond to the psychological functions of Thinking, Sensation Intuition and Feeling. Her classical god-forms include Demeter and Gaea.

The moon is usually considered as feminine, as three-fold goddess in her three phases of waxing, full and waning. In one aspect she is the dark Hecate of witchcraft and spells; in another the virgin huntress Diana/Artemis, with particular guardianship over pregnancy and the young. She is also Isis, wandering through the skies looking for her lost lover, Osiris. The Moon rules over the tides, not only physically in the tides of the sea, but all the inner tides of organic growth and psychic ebb and flow.

Mercury is representative of trade, commerce, trickery, communication, science, magic and indeed all knowledge. In terms of ancient civilisations he is seen as the Roman Mercury, the Greek Hermes, and as the Egyptian Thoth – the ibis-headed scribe of the gods, lord of books and learning.

Venus is connected with love and desire. The counterparts of the Roman Venus are the Greek Aphrodite, and the Babylonian Ishtar, from whose worship and mysteries comes the dance of the seven veils – which in its deeper significance is rather more than an erotic pagan cabaret.

The Sun is of course the major luminary and is representative of gods of Light. As the swing of the earth and sun bring the seasons of the year, and the more frequent cycle of days and nights, we have also the hero and saviour gods who save their people from death and darkness. Amongst these are the Greek Apollo, the Egyptian Osiris and the Scandinavian Balder the Beautiful.

Mars is associated with the disciplining forces of war and restriction: the wrath of the gods. Thor, the Norse thunder-god, can be found here, along with the Roman Mars and the Greek Ares; although at root they have a less bellicose aspect, as agricultural gods, or smiths, who taught men the forging of metals and the use of tools.

Jupiter is more beneficent, indicative of more peaceful and stable conditions, of rule and law. All god-kings sit here, such as the Greek Zeus and his consort Hera. Most of the gods have goddess counterparts.

Saturn is concerned with wisdom, as opposed to the knowledge of Mercury, and has connections with older gods, such as Cronos, the Father of Zeus. One might even put father-gods in connection with Jupiter, grandfather gods with Saturn. There is a traditional linking of these planetary categories according with the ages of man, as cited by Shakespeare.

Shakespeare also speaks of the 'music of the spheres'. These spheres are not the planetary spheres in the way that we think of them today, but rather concentric crystalline spheres surrounding the earth upon the surface of which each planet can be found.

When one reached the crystalline sphere of Saturn, there was a further one, of the Fixed Stars. The Fixed Stars are usually char-

The Crystalline Spheres

acterised by the Zodiac, which is that belt of constellations before which the planets, in their relatively flat associated orbits, appear to pass when viewed from the Earth. The Zodiac is divided into twelve sectors which are the traditional zodiacal signs – Aries the Ram, etc.

The crystalline sphere of the Fixed Stars also turns apparently on an axis more or less equivalent (in our times at least) to Polaris, the Pole Star. Celestial sky-gods such as Uranus can be associated with it, though there is a beautiful image from Celtic mythology which sees it as the turning glass castle of Arianrod.

Finally, beyond all, is the clear sphere which has no luminaries upon it, but which, under the title of *Primum Mobile*, furnishes the source of movement for all the interior spheres.

By means of a classification system such as this we are able to come to grips with the teeming profusions and apparent chaos of the myths and legends of mankind.

This is not entirely an exercise in the history of ancient ideas. The pagan gods do not have to be dug for in the dark recesses of the mind. They shout at us from every advertisement hoarding, from the cinema screen, video and television set.

There we see hero gods, war gods, sex goddesses, acting out their immemorial relationships. Man is still being entertained and preoccupied with the projected contents of his own soul mirrored back to him – now by electronic media and paperback novel as once by the bard.

Time was when these projections of the human psyche, of the interior universe, were thought to be actual representations of the outer universe. Medieval man could really believe that the earth was surrounded by crystalline spheres that had to pushed round by invisible angelic beings.

However, with the scientific revolution it was found that the outer universe did not accord with man's interior projections and preconceptions. Eventually, when scientific truth finally won through, it resulted in the old ideas being discarded as mere superstition. This is a pity, for though they may have made poor physics and astronomy, they make very good psychology and social anthropology. And as committed occultists would maintain, there is even yet more to it than this!

For the whole universe cannot be reduced to psychological complexes buzzing around in our heads. In other words, there *are* also objective spiritual beings in the worlds about us, who share our universe.

4 HERMES AND THE PAGAN MYSTERIES
The origins of the occult

It will help us to get things into perspective if we survey the history of religious and scientific ideas, particularly as they apply to magic, from the time of the Renaissance.

Magic is here not a convention in childrens' fairy stories, but a means of operating upon one level of nature by manipulating another level. The mechanics of this are worked out by the theory of 'correspondences' or 'occult sympathies', the idea being that by working upon symbols one may have an effect upon that which they represent.

There are different degrees of symbols. Written words upon a page are convenient signs for realities. The symbolism used in the occult arts is however of a deeper kind, and wells up from the unconscious mind.

A Florentine priest, physician and scholar named Marsilio Ficino (1433–1499) is a key figure here. It is he who was given the task of translating the Hermetic literature from the Greek. The rediscovery of the riches of the classical world had only recently occurred.

When the Greek texts became available it was Ficino's appointed task to translate them, with particular emphasis on the works of Plato. Before he could do this some other texts came to light which were held to be more important even than the works of Plato. This was the Hermetic literature.

The Hermetic literature was so called because it purported to be written by a high priest of ancient Egypt named Hermes Trismegistus (Hermes Thrice-greatest). It was considered to be highly important because it was believed to be older than the works of Plato, and to be contemporaneous with the writings of Moses in the Old Testament. It was generally thought, that in very ancient times, there had been a golden age of great knowledge, peace and wisdom, an Edenic state. Therefore any manuscript of great age was to be highly regarded. This was particularly so in the case of the Hermes literature because it seemed to foreshadow and prophesy the decline of Egyptian magic and religion, and to foretell the coming of the Christian era, using very similar terms to those in the Gospel of St. John.

In fact this prophetic element was not so remarkable as at first appeared. The Hermes literature was actually of a comparatively late date. Far from being contemporary with the writing of the Old Testament it was in fact written in about the first to third centuries A.D. This was not discovered until the textual researches of Isaac Casaubon in 1614 and, until this date, the Hermes literature held a very high place in academic and even religious thought.

However, the Hermetic tradition is still very important in its own right, for it represents a fusion of early Christian thought with the best of the old pagan traditions. It was a belief of more enlightened and liberal Christians that the new religious teachings came, as Jesus said, not to destroy the old law, but to fulfil it. This was held to apply to the old pagan beliefs as well as to the Jewish Old Testament law.

Early church fathers, such as Lanctantius, were particularly sympathetic to this idea.

There are in fact three streams of Christian thought. On one side is the tendency to underrate and even condemn the pagan insights. This is broadly the main stream of Christian orthodoxy.

On the other side is the tendency to overplay the pagan contribution. This found expression in Gnosticism, a complex system of thought that substituted angelologies for pantheons of gods and spirits.

The stream that runs between these two is the Hermetic tradition, and it is probable that this too would have succumbed to the pressures of orthodox Christian thought, but for two historical accidents.

The first, which we have already mentioned, is the supposed great antiquity that lent authority to the Hermetic tradition and caused it to be respected by theologians of the period.

The other was theological support for it in the work of a writer whom we nowadays refer to as pseudo-Dionysius. He was however, in those days, by no means regarded as pseudo, but taken at face value, as Dionysius the Areopagite, mentioned in the New Testament as a close companion of St. Paul. In fact the writings of Dionysius date from about the same time as the Hermetic literature and are indeed a product of much the same confluence of ideas.

The Hermetic writings and those of pseudo-Dionysius received the support of theologians as eminent as Thomas Aquinas in spite of the fact that they also formed the basis for certain debased forms of medieval magic.

Some of the atmosphere of the pagan world of the times can be gleaned from a popular work of the period, *The Golden Ass* of Apuleius. This scurrilous and highly amusing work is written by one who was an initiate of the Mysteries of Isis, and from this book the imaginative reader can get a fine grasp of the spiritual side of pagan religion as well as of its more superstitious and debased side.

The pagan mystery tradition sprang up in about the third century B.C. possibly as a result, and certainly stimulated by, the conquests of Alexander the Great.

Alexander, in becoming master of the known world and using a cosmopolitan army, spread a common language – *koine*, or common Greek – across the face of the world. This caused a great synthesising movement in the religions of the time.

Gods and goddesses that had been local to particular isolated city-states, or to tribes or nations, found themselves cheek by jowl with one another, particularly in large cities. They then discovered that they had much in common one with another.

This had two results. One was that the sanctions of morality and loyalty strengthened by a national system of gods tended to be weakened. As a replacement for this one saw the development of the Imperial cult. This is better known to us in its later Roman manifestations of power-drunk emperors, but the first of the Imperial human-god rulers was Alexander. The citizen's first duty was to the Emperor god; after that one could worship as one liked. Naturally this would tend to be the gods of one's fathers. But there was no stigma, apart from local traditions, in worshipping any gods one wished. There was in fact a very considerable degree of religious tolerance.

There also developed a deeper spiritual and philosophical element. It became of concern to those who thought a little deeper that there should be some unifying principle behind the great multiplicity of

gods and goddesses. With so many divine contenders where was the
One True God of the Universe? Where, and who, was the divine
counterpart of the earthly Alexander?

This brought about a synthesising religious philosophy that saw all
the gods as manifestations of the One God. That which one
worshipped in Apollo, was the same Supreme Being whom others
worshipped in the form of Horus, or Ishtar.

The pagan mysteries that developed from this trend became great
international religious centres, such as Eleusis. Here the Mysteries of
Demeter were celebrated which retained the secrecy of their rites in
spite of their immense popularity. There were other Mystery cults,
such as those of Isis – about which Apuleius, author of *The Golden
Ass* – gave some hints and later there were those of Mithra.

We can, to a fair extent, reconstruct the nature and purpose of
these 'Mystery' cults in spite of the vows of secrecy that were
imposed, for they embodied psychological knowledge and religious
intent that would be regarded as part of the occult today.

The secrecy was imposed for very good reason. It was necessary, for
the work to be effective, that the candidate to the Mysteries enter
into an 'Unknown' situation – just as the soul enters the unknown at
physical death.

Bound and blindfolded he would shamble his impromptu way
through a part in a ritual drama. The other protagonists represented
great powers or forces within the soul, in the guise of various pagan
gods, according to the type of Mystery being performed. The gist of
the drama would be that of death and then joyous rebirth – which
the neophyte would either undergo himself or witness in the person
of a main character in the drama.

Thus in the Mysteries of Demeter, her daughter Persephone would
be seized and carried down to Hades by Pluto while her mother
mourned her loss, until her eventual return.

In the Mysteries of Isis and Osiris, Osiris is murdered by his
adversary Set and cut up and dispersed, after which his mourning
consort Isis searches for his dismembered body and he is eventually
miraculously restored, and avenged by his son Horus.

We should say that there is much more to such ritual performances
than may be apparent in our bald descriptions of them. They are
called Mysteries in much the same sense that the Roman Catholic
church defines a Mystery today – as a truth beyond the reach of
reason.

It is very easy to look upon such 'Mysteries' in a shallow and cerebral way and to regard them as childish fantasies that try to give some hope of the soul's survival after death. They are in fact much more than this. If the soul is transcendent and immortal then an enactment of imaginative intensity that brings a conscious realisation of that fact is a step toward the truth rather than a delusion.

Also there is more to 'childish fantasy' than may be supposed. According to Coleridge, one of the great religious thinkers of the past two hundred years, the imagination is one of the great pointers to reality for man. It is his creative part that enables him to survive and progress, the counterpart of the *Fiat Lux* at the creation of the universe.

It is not our task to analyse Coleridge's theory of the imagination, except to say that, from an occult point of view, it is borne out. This is indeed summed up in a traditional saying: "Fantasy is the ass that carries the ark".

In other words, by taking the imagination seriously, beyond the level of mere personal fantasy, it tends to structure itself according to archetypal patterns. It is this that gives the perennial appeal to the old myths and legends; the appeal of the Round Table of King Arthur and his Knights, for instance; of the High History of the Holy Grail, and so on.

5 FREUD, JUNG AND THE SCIENTIFIC METHOD
Approaches to the occult

Freud is on record as having said to Jung that he was afraid of psychoanalysis being swamped by a 'black mud' of occultism. One may sympathise with his fears. Any field of investigation that places imagination and intuition to the fore rather than intellect and sense perception, is open to abuse and distortion from much uncorroborated fantasy. There are considerably more asses that do not carry 'arks' than those that do! The lunatic fringe of occultism is perpetual witness of this danger.

However, one does not solve problems by ignoring them and Jung found it necessary to go his own way. Abandoning Freud's conceptions, he accepted the fantasies of the unconscious as he found them, without imposing rigid sexual theories upon them. He maintained that the fantasies, either of dream or of the waking imagination, could be pointers to a re-integration of the personality, and have an objective reality of their own.

Here we come across an old problem of philosophy. Where does the subjective end and the objective begin?

Jung was aware of this problem and indeed speaks forcefully of the 'objectivity' of the unconscious. In his autobiography, *Memories, Dreams, Reflections* he cites the case of 'Philemon'. Philemon was a fantasy character he first met in a dream – a horned but human figure with kingfisher wings. Shortly after this vivid dream he found a dead kingfisher on a country walk – a rare and highly coincidental event.

Philemon then began turning up with considerable force in his waking thoughts and conversing in a way that was completely 'other' than Jung's own ideas and thought processes. At one point the pressure came upon him to write this material down, and while this pressure was building up his house started to manifest symptoms of 'haunting'. There was a heavy brooding atmosphere, doors slammed, bells rang, his daughter saw an apparition. Everything cleared when the book was written.

Whatever the objective or subjective reality of 'Philemon', these events were crucial in Jung's career. He felt that but for the 'earthing' provided by his work, his wife and family, he might well have lost his reason at this time, and his whole life's work stems from this critical period. He came to look upon 'Philemon' as a discarnate guru, or spiritual teacher – a concept relatively common in the Orient but little recognised in the West.

Approaches to the occult can be on various levels and take on various forms. The theory of coincidence (as, for example, with the kingfisher) is developed by Jung in *Synchronicity – An Acausal Connecting Principle*, written in collaboration with the mathematician C.W. Pauli.

Other occult investigators have concentrated upon dreaming of the future. Any who care to read *An Experiment With Time* by W.J. Dunne may themselves undertake the experiment and see if they too dream of the future.

At another level are those who would have been keener to investigate the bells, raps and apparitions that Jung experienced with recording apparatus and all the paraphernalia of psychical research. But such approaches – of the intellect and the senses – only scratch at the surface of deep areas of experience that do not succumb to investigations of this type. Unless we are prepared to train the imagination and intuition, nothing will be achieved in the pursuit of occult studies.

It may be felt that the occult tradition has done little to benefit the human race. In fact the whole of our scientific method started as a new attitude of mind that manifested itself first in Renaissance magic. It is taken for granted in our own day, and sees man as an active influence on the universe around him.

The medieval view regarded man as a part of God's creation, in which he suffered the results of a Fall from Grace as described in the Old Testament. It followed that he had but to accept the situation, at the same time striving for moral virtue in the light of Divine Grace.

Getting oneself right with the Creator was considered of greater importance than tinkering with parts of the Creation in order to make it a more comfortable place to live in. To get on good terms with the landlord and hope for a transfer to a better place.

It is possible that today, we have gone too far the other way, and spend so much time and effort in improving our planetary accommodation that we have rather forgotten about God, or the landlord.

This may account for the fact that, in spite of all our undoubted improvements the benefits of such are still unfairly spread throughout the world. We are also in danger of exhausting the mineral heritage of the earth and polluting ourselves into extinction.

The re-awakening interest in the 'inner worlds', and concern for the environment, may show an increasing realisation that somewhere along the line, in recent centuries, we took a wrong turning. That wrong turning may have been the separation of science and technology from a religious and moral context.

6 NATURAL AND CELESTIAL MAGIC
A methodology of the occult

When Ficino started to investigate 'natural magic', the structure of the universe as he saw it had already been defined by scholastic philosophy. Through a tradition of such great systematic thinkers as Thomas Aquinas, a poet of the genius of Dante could present it in poetic art. Ficino was a keen student of Dante and we would do well to examine just what they actually believed, for it has a considerable effect on much that has followed.

Ficino, as translator for Cosimo de Medici, had the task of translating the Hermetic literature from the Greek, and this was considered so important that it took precedence even over the works of Plato. We have already mentioned some of the reasons for this high regard.

There had always been a debased kind of Hermeticism: an illiterate mass of witchcraft and old folk remedies. Some of it no doubt good folk medicine but also containing much superstition, barbarous beliefs and practices. Ficino felt that his work of translation would help restore such fallen and debased ideas to their true pinnacle as a high form of human knowledge.

Ficino was a doctor, as well as priest and translator, and his magical ideas took shape as part of a medical treatise. What he advocated would be rated harmless enough today, perhaps even psychologically beneficial, but he had to be careful not to offend ecclesiastical prejudices.

He advocated the use of colour and sound as a way of counter-balancing any tendency to mental imbalance. This was in the context of a planetary classification of man's psychology and environment.

Thus if a scholar had a tendency to melancholia, Ficino would say he was suffering, (by the over-application of his type of work) from a surfeit of influences pertaining to Saturn. To counteract this, Ficino advocated that he deliberately surround himself periodically with the influences of less melancholic celestial bodies, such as Jupiter, Venus or the Sun.

This could be achieved by wandering in the fields on sunny days or when the morning or evening star was in the sky, picking flowers attributed to Sol or Venus, or one could set up an artificial environment in a private room.

In this room one would have lamps representing the various planets, arranged according to one's needs, together with appropriate flowers, decorations and colours. Then one would play and sing suitable planetary hymns, the words taken from traditional Orphic Hymns, which Ficino had translated. The melodies were also composed upon certain symbolic conventions appropriate to the planets.

Ficino was at great pains to point out that this was *natural* magic, that it simply made use of the correspondence between various natural forces, and thus had no area of conflict with the claims of religion. To support his views in case he should be charged with heresy, he also marshalled the evidence of Aquinas, Lanctantius and any who had written favourably of the Hermes literature, including the pseudo-Dionysius.

His caution paid off in that he was not so charged; but there were others, less inhibited, who rushed into the gateway that he had opened. One of the most important of these was Pico della Mirandola, a brilliant Renaissance prince, who had studied systematically all the known philosophies. He proposed, at the age of twenty-four, a synthesis of them, which he offered to defend in public debate, in Rome.

Pico was a student of Hebrew, and had studied the 'secret wisdom' of the Jews, who had an oral mystical/magical tradition that was compiled and written down by Moses de Leon in 1305. This compilation was called the *Zohar*, or *Book of Splendour*, and together with an early work called the *Book of Formation*, or *Sepher Yetzirah*, is the foundation of this system. The system is called the *Qabalah*, from the Hebrew word QBL ('to receive') as the teaching was traditionally conveyed from mouth to ear. The Qabalistic teaching had many leaders and developers, such as Abraham Abalufia, but it is not our purpose to trace its descent through purely Jewish traditions but to discuss its effect upon the Christian world of the time.

The Jewish stream, important though it may have been to Jewry, did not have a major impact on Western Europe, but its Christianised off-shoots did – if in a somewhat different form.

The contribution that Pico della Mirandola made to the natural magic of Ficino was to introduce two further levels to it. Whereas Ficino was content with the planetary or celestial correspondences that could be drawn up in relation to natural objects, Pico, from the Qabalah, introduced angelic correspondences to all the planets and stars, and beyond that, correspondences to aspects of God Himself. Naturally this was not taken lightly by the ecclesiastical authorities.

Today Ficino's magic could be looked upon as efficacious upon a psychological level. After a course of meditation that fixed in the mind associations between various symbols, colours, sounds, objects, emotions, and so on, further meditation in surroundings that accentuate them would concentrate the mind to a higher degree than normal. This can have an out-of-the-ordinary effect upon consciousness. We have, of recent years, received reports of experiments in sensory deprivation in connection with space research; what we have in Ficino's magic is a sensory *concentration* upon one particular range of experience.

As an example of the traditional field of correspondences, or sympathies, let us take the planet Jupiter. An application of Ficino's magic would concentrate upon the colour deep blue; the principle of mercy, rulership and magnanimity; the amethyst or sapphire; the olive; the shamrock; the centaur; cedar perfume or incense; the wand, sceptre, or shepherd's crook; any solid geometric figure but principally the tetrahedron; the equal-armed cross; tin; the zodiacal sign Sagittarius; the image of a crowned and throned king; the number four; the digestive system; gout; and so on. A little examination will show that these are not completely arbitrary choices but follow upon a basic traditional motif.

Such attributions are not tightly fixed, but nor are they completely arbitrary. There is a level of the mind that sorts out the relatedness and relevance of objects used as symbols. It is an intuitive and emotional level rather than intellectual and deals with images and feelings rather than ideas.

From a catalogue such as we have made in relation to Jupiter it can easily be imagined that a formal ceremony with relevant symbolic objects could be made, that would ably concentrate the mind in a particular direction. One could even go to less trouble and simply sit in a quiet and darkened room and meditate upon such symbols, given a modicum of training in meditation technique.

7 GROUP MINDS AND MASS MEDIA
The social impact of the occult

From the experience of those who have practical knowledge of occultism, effects upon the mind are greatly increased when there is more than one person present. Some go so far as to posit a kind of square rule, or geometric progression, as to the psychological power generated. That is, two people generate four times the effect of one, three people nine times, and so on. We would not quantify it so precisely, as obviously much will depend upon the subjective condition of those present. There also seems to be an optimum practical number for any working group, between about seven and thirteen. To have less means that personal factors still obtrude in the working of the whole, whereas to have more makes the situation somewhat less flexible and even psychologically 'stodgy'.

In this we are moving into the psychology of the group. This ranges from the pioneering *Instincts of the Herd in Peace and War* by Trotter, to the considerable corpus of work on the group mind by Jung.

There is a tradition in occult circles that Hitler and his associates were steeped in occultism of a dubious kind – what would popularly be called 'Black Magic'. Certainly they were pioneers of the psychological manipulation of masses. The dramatic effects of the Nuremberg rallies and the semi-mystical aura deliberately developed about the banners, the party symbols and the Fuhrer indicates that we are close to the principles of Ficino's 'natural magic', if a perversion of them.

Goebbels also realised that such methods could be extended to the media of radio and film. Indeed, in the cinema and television, with a

group of people sitting in relative quiet and darkness, their attention
fixed on a bright screen upon which images are flashed, we have a
device which would have overjoyed Ficino and the other Renaissance
magicians as a magical instrument of great power.

We would do well to ponder to what extent we affect ourselves by
such devices. The gods of old are the very stuff of popular entertainment. Some war and even cowboy films could hardly be better
constructed rituals of Mars, and other types of film leave few aspects
of the cult of Aphrodite unexplored. International female stars have
clearly taken on the attributes of the goddess. The larger-than-life
eccentricity that has become a tradition of show business has some
relation to an inflation of the psyche due to focussed mob adulation.
One may call this an aspect of psychology, but it is also within the
province of magic as properly understood.

Magic, according to the definition of one modern exponent, Dion
Fortune, is the art of causing changes in consciousness in accordance
with will.

This is as ordinary or extraordinary as one likes to make it. It may
simply be a changing of mood by appropriate music, symbols,
colours or lights – either in oneself or others. This may seem
relatively harmless, and even obvious, but it is a jumping-off-point to
other states of consciousness.

Instilling fear, and the belief that some unknown force will be
actively working against the life or property of the victim is one of
the darker aspects of sorcery or witchcraft. This is no 'mere
superstition' to the primitive mind – natives can be actually killed by
it.

There were real grounds for the anti-witch hysteria in Western
Europe. Deplorable though the savagery of much 'witch-hunting'
may have been, there is another side to it – the genuine fears of a type
of evil or wonder-working against which there was no known
defence.

The piercing of a wax doll with pins or nails, or the unravelling of a
piece of red wool as its "life thread" – almost always with the
knowledge of the intended victim – may seem as childish games to
well integrated modern minds, but the motivation is the same as the
use of actual physical weapons, and induced fears and phobias are not
to be lightly dismissed.

In discussing witchcraft we should distinguish between the popular
use of the term as the craft of ancient evil workers, and its use

nowadays by the neo-pagan movement, who equate it with the craft of "the wise".

Today's neo-pagan movement is more a religious than an occult phenomenon, and is a possible reaction against an institutionalised Christian church, on the one hand, and an institutionalised urban society on the other. It is a generally laudable "back to nature" movement reviving old folklore and legends and seeking religious experience in Nature. It is a celebration of the Old Religion – pre-Christian Western paganism – rather than witchcraft, even if many of its adherents call themselves witches.

To return to the general psychology of magic, we see that a genuine belief in the *deeper* powers possible can well bring about deeper and wider-ranging effects than a mere temporary change of mood.

There is no doubt that Ficino felt more effect from the appropriate planetary colours and symbols than we might do. First because he had formed, by intellectual effort, a connection between them. Secondly because he firmly *believed* it as a fact of nature.

Intellectual connections may be discovered by us moderns if we are prepared to research into the lore of ancient times. But belief does not come so easily. We live in disbelieving times, with more faith in our own technological cleverness than in any deeper side to existence.

The occult appears as an escapist abrogation of intellect only to those who are too thoroughly steeped in the pre-conceptions of our own age.

We strike deeper issues with the addition of Pico della Mirandola's Qabalistic Magic to the Natural Magic of Marsilio Ficino. This led to a formulation of a three-tier universe exemplified by the study of Occult Philosophy in three branches, one above the other. These were Theology, Mathematics and Physics.

The occult study of Theology is not only that of man's knowledge of God as understood in academic theology, but also the way that God *continues* to act within the Universe through the powers of celestial beings or spirits.

The occult study of Mathematics is not just the rationalistic study it is today but an attempt to define the archetypal principles behind form, the 'quality' of numbers, and the 'inner' laws that govern events in the world.

The occult study of Physics is not simply a branch of physical science but a study of the inner sympathies with all aspects of nature, and bearing in mind the occult mathematical and theological linkages.

None of this would cut much ice in current academic disciplines but it should not be dismissed out of hand for that. It is plain that our technological civilisation has not solved all the problems of the universe yet!

Although in general academic traditions and standards are high, there are still limitations and blind spots caused by political and social pressures, and even by fashion. An academic needs to be brave to investigate an area that seems to be out of the general run of 'respectable' research. There has also been, until recently, an extremely limiting degree of specialisation. From all this it is possible for certain matters to have dropped from academic concern, not because they have been disproved but because they have been forgotten.

When truths are neglected they tend to spring up in all kinds of 'unofficial' forms, whether in the scientific or religious field. They are generally seized upon by the formally unqualified ('dropped out' subjects tend naturally to attract 'dropped out' people) and this serves further to alienate 'official' opinion and standards.

We are not saying that all the 'dropped out' subjects are worthy of reclamation or are repositories of great truths, any more than 'dropped out' people are all shining intellects rising above their age. But just as one can have the occasional brilliant intellect, who is unable to fit into the preconceptions of his own generation, so is it possible to have a subject-area discredited because it does not fit into current preconceptions.

Occultism, in one sense, is a refuse-heap of rejected knowledge that will not stay rejected. Therefore much of it bears re-examination from time to time in the light of new insights and understandings. Such new insights may be gained in subject-areas as diverse as mystical theology, psycho-analysis, mathematics, archeology, psychology, pharmacology, social anthropology and even the physical sciences.

In the light of modern historical scholarship (such as Frances Yates' *Giordano Bruno and the Hermetic Tradition, The Rosicrucian Enlightenment* etc.), we can see how some of this rejection of 'occult' subjects came about.

Originally the 'magical' *impulse* was very much the same as the 'scientific'. It was the declared aim of Trithemius of Sponheim, for example, to build a vast communications system across the known world, only he advocated angelic and psychical means whereas we have now done the same thing by physical technology. Whilst giving all due credit to the development of telecommunications we should not at the same time entirely discredit the angelic and the psychical.

There was indeed no rigid dividing-line between what we now regard as occult subjects and the physical sciences. Great thinkers and scientists of the past (Elias Ashmole, Roger Bacon, Giordano Bruno, Tycho Brahe, Kepler, Halley and even Isaac Newton) easily encompassed both.

8 VISIONS OF THE MILLENIUM
The power behind the occult

Before we had this great technological upsurge as a panacea for all ills, mankind's discontent with his lot tended to be expressed in religious terms. Things were bad and uncomfortable, they always *had* been bad and uncomfortable, and always *were* going to be bad and uncomfortable. The only real hope was the End of the World, or, failing that, the Dawning of a New Age.

This kind of eschatological hope had, like the religious traditions of Europe, come originally from the Jews. Since the great days of the Kingdom of David (about 1000 B.C.) there had always been the hope of a Messiah who would come and institute a world order, a new age of justice, and harmony, a kind of New Eden.

To the practical Jewish mind, which has the characteristic of being very down-to-earth at the same time as being capable of high metaphysical flights, this meant just that: a real physical world order and nothing unworldly or symbolic about it. This found concrete expression in the revolt of Judas Maccabeus, and by no means the last one either, although better known to the Gentile world because of its Biblical context.

Professor Norman Cohn in *The Pursuit of the Millennium* has delineated many of the popular religious movements of the Middle Ages, and shown the connections between millenarial hopes and heresies and the first stirrings of a proletarian social and political movement. This religious revolutionary fervour surfaces again and again until its eventual secularisation in the eighteenth-century, culminating in the French and American Revolutions.

One of the great Christian Millenarial movements foresaw the start of a New Age in 1260. This even had the acknowledgement of the Popes of the time, partly because of the convincing case put for it by Joachim de Floris, a Calabrian visionary.

By calculations based on Biblical chronology he divided the history of the world into an Age of the Father, an Age of the Son, and an Age of the Holy Spirit. The first age had been under the fear of God, and the Old Law of the Old Testament; the second under the love of God, and pertaining to the New Testament and the rise of Christianity; while the third age would be under the power and inspiration of the Holy Spirit, who would overturn the corruption of the world and bring all to judgement and renewal.

Here was a great complex of tangled threads of hopes and traditions. Discontent with the church rumbled on until the Protestant churches broke away from Rome. The beginnings of this could be seen in the thirteenth century when the whole of Germany was placed under an interdict, and the church officially withdrew from all religious functions such as baptism, marriages, and burials. This left the way open for monks and friars, and even laymen and self-appointed prophets, to preach to the people, usually in a way very critical of the clerical hierarchy.

An earlier mass movement was the phenomenon of the first Crusade, perhaps the first ever popular international movement.

There were many political and social reasons for there to be a popular response to the preaching for the Crusade by Pope Urban II in 1095. The Pope himself found it a great opportunity to exert influence in the East. The Great Schism between the Roman Catholic Church and the Greek Orthodox church centred in Byzantium, had comparatively recently occurred, in 1054. The encroachment of Turkish hordes upon the great Christian city of the East eventually forced the Emperor Michael Comnenis to appeal to Rome. This must have seemed almost like divine intervention and holy vindication for the Papacy.

The response to his preaching for a Crusade was overwhelming. The Norman aristocracy found it appealing because, through their system of primogeniture, a father's property went to his eldest son. This meant that there was a whole class of land-hungry younger brothers. They welcomed a chance to hew out lands for themselves in the Near East.

As for the ordinary people, their response was even more enthusiastic and stemmed largely from their poverty. But there was a great deal more to their enthusiasm than a desire for emigration, and the saving of Jerusalem became invested with a charismatic glow. This is strange, for Jerusalem had been in the hands of the Turks for centuries, having fallen to the Caliph Omar in the early days of Islamic expansion in 638.

The whole thing became a religious and New Age quest, with the Turks seen as demonic agents and the Crusaders as the blessed Elect who would save the city of God from evil, and usher in an age of a New Jerusalem. Popular preachers, such as Peter the Hermit, incited the common people to go on the great holy war of divine liberation. The Church encouraged volunteers for the Crusades by giving protection to the property of all who went and by promising them forgiveness of sins and a sure place in Heaven should they fall in battle in the Divine cause.

The effects grew out of hand. A great rabble began moving towards the East, the People's Crusade, a full year before a properly equipped military expedition, comprised of knights and soldiers, could be got under way.

The beginnings of this popular movement were not edifying. They persecuted Jews on the way, as part of their Christian mission. And mistaking Bulgarian Christians for heathens, massacred them too. The Emperor of Byzantium, when he saw this vast rabble at his gates, pillaging and looting to sustain themselves, transported them across the Bosphorus in short order, where soon afterward they were massacred by the Turks. Those few who escaped death were taken into slavery, never to be seen again.

The Crusades are very important to any survey of the occult in the West. They represent a great popular movement motivated by 'inner' or non-physical considerations. A great 'New Age' movement, an inner urge of the soul, projected outwards onto physical circumstances.

Another important fact about the crusades is that they brought a major influx of ideas into Europe. When the Islamic religion was founded the Arabs, with a new religion to give impetus to their expansion, had swept on to conquer lands as far away as India and China. They absorbed all the ideas and sciences they encountered and built up a great body of learning while Europe was still in the Dark Ages.

Algebra for instance, is an Arabic word, and we owe much of our mathematics to them, particularly the concept of zero. They were

also responsible for the science of Alchemy, which was the foundation of the chemical sciences of today.

There was already some cultural interchange through the channels
of trade, but the confrontation of the Crusades brought about a
deeper and more fruitful exchange. This was aided by the practice of
holding knights and nobles for ransom. Some were kept in Arab
custody for years and learned much of the Arabic culture.

On the occult and religious side this led to a number of movements
that profoundly affected Western culture. Amongst them were the
cult of Courtly Love, the guilds of 'free masons' who were responsible for the sudden in-rush of the Gothic style of architecture, the
military-religious chivalry of the Knights Templar and Knights
Hospitaller, and the Holy Grail legends.

Courtly Love has close connections with England, for the Queen
of the Troubador Minstrelsy was Eleanor of Aquitaine, the remarkable mother of Kings Richard I and John. She married first the King
of France and then Henry Plantagenet, who became Henry II.

It is difficult to trace its origins. William of Poitier, the first
recorded Troubador, died in 1137, and Richard I was connected
with the movement, at least in legend, by Blondel seeking his
imprisoned master by playing and singing beneath prison towers
throughout all Europe.

Ostensibly it was simply a courtly convention in which young men
composed verse and song praising their lady-love in superlative
terms, placing her on a romantic pedestal and descanting about the
agony of unrequited love. The loved one was never one's spouse, nor
ever became so, but it would be a mistake to consider it to be simply
a movement of moral laxity. There were rigid rules and conventions
by which this troubador passion was expressed and received. This
ranged from 'looking', to the ultimate 'the giving of thanks', and
there were generally seven stages of approach to the beloved.

The adoration of a lady and an approach to her by seven stages
suggests that behind Courtly Love was a goddess cult that probably
came from the Near East, as a result of the Crusades. There is a close
parallel with the seven stages of Sufi mysticism, and though that
mysticism is turned toward Allah, the divine love poems of the Sufi
mystics are couched in terms that are as erotic as the *Song of Solomon*
in the Bible.

Contemporary with this movement was the concern of the church
with heresy. In the period from about 1100 to 1300, we see a

considerable increase in the regard held for the Blessed Virgin Mary, as a counter to any heretical tendency towards a Queen Venus.

The period also saw the foundation of the Dominican Order, who, besides being teachers, have been dubbed 'hunters of heresy'; also the beginning of the Inquisition. One Crusade during this period was directed not at the Infidel Moor but at the region of Albi in the South of France, where a dualistic heresy had sprung up.

The Knights Templar, one of the two main orders of warrior monks who had been formed soon after the First Crusade, ostensibly to keep open the pilgrim routes, were steeped in secret rites and traditions and were finally dissolved for alleged heresy. There were political reasons for so doing, but nonetheless there was something about them that disturbed the religious orthodoxy of the times.

We get some hint of it by the Order's close association with the Temple of Solomon at Jerusalem, from which, indeed, they derived their name. The ritual and secret teachings of Freemasonry are also based upon the measurement of Solomon's Temple, which is described with considerable numerological and symbolical exactitude in the Old Testament.

To this we may ally the sudden upspringings of Gothic Architecture by the 'free masons' and it has even been suggested that the money for such projects – and the number of huge gothic structures throughout France, even at the most unprepossessing places – came from alchemical gold, fantastic though this may sound. Whatever one may choose to believe or disbelieve in the fascinating web of conjecture that has grown up about this period, we may plainly claim that this is the stuff of occultism.

We have defined occultism as rejected science and religion. There is much that is hidden and rejected here, including a rejected or lost technology. The canon, based on the Pythagorean Golden Mean, by which Gothic architecture was developed, is worthy of some examination, being the exemplification of occult design and occult mathematics.

9   THE RISE OF TECHNOLOGY
The 'occultation' of the occult

The first blow to prestige received by the Hermetic Tradition was from the textual criticism of Isaac Casaubon who proved that it was not of vast antiquity. Thus, what had seemed miraculously prophetic in it was in fact but a record of that which was past. On the theological front there was a similar re-dating of the works alleged to be by Dionysius the Areopagite. The church authorities lost little time in degrading the Hermetic Tradition and all that went with it.

However, Hermeticism acted as a buffer between the contending forces of the Reformation. The skein of events and opinions is tangled, yet the occult plays an important role in the history of the Reformation and the development of the scientific method.

The 'occult' attitude of mind saw man as an enquiring investigator of nature, and initiated the scientific method. This is the origin of the Faust legend. Was man seeking forbidden knowledge? Was this attitude of mind a re-enactment of the disobedience in the Garden of Eden? The medieval mind would have thought so. The awakening magical mind saw it rather as a step forward in the cosmic significance of man. One of Pico della Mirandola's great theses was called *The Dignity of Man*.

The developing confrontation between the Reformation and Counter-Reformation saw a body of liberal thinkers, (including Sir Philip Sidney and Sir Thomas More), who became students of a philosophical religious Hermeticism that sought a middle way between the conflicting forces.

In her study, *The Rosicrucian Enlightenment*, Frances Yates gives evidence for the later development of this movement in the attempt to make the state of Bohemia into a buffer between Protestant and Catholic forces. This was the political basis of the Rosicrucian Manifestos of the early seventeenth-century that made such an impact in their day. They announced the existence of a secret brotherhood of magical adepts who sought to bring peace and wisdom to the world.

The state of Bohemia had a drastically short existence and fell into ruins and the Rosicrucian movement continued as an intellectual rather than a political movement. Its main protagonists in the later seventeenth-century were Robert Fludd and the Jesuit Athanasius Kircher, who represent the last flowering of the occult approach to knowledge before it disappears underground, not to re-appear significantly until our own day.

The intellectual event of real importance in the later seventeenth-century was the formation of the Royal Society, when the scientific investigation of nature received royal patronage. Even so, it met with severe criticism and religious pressures, and for this reason the Royal Society sought not to espouse any field of study that might lead to confrontation with religious authority. These included alchemy, astrology and other occult sciences. Yet these remained of considerable interest to scientists such as Newton, Elias Ashmole and Kepler.

But the expediency of not jeopardising the reputation of science by avoiding confrontation with religion, plus the practical results of a growing technology, were sufficient for the occult arts and sciences to go into a decline, and they followed an underground course through most of the eighteenth and nineteenth centuries.

At the end of the eighteenth century there was an attempted resurgence by Thomas Taylor, who was a stalwart defender of ancient philosophy and science and who translated the works of Plato, Proclus and other ancients into English. He had a considerable effect upon the romantic poets of the early nineteenth century: Blake, Coleridge, Wordsworth, and upon Emerson and the New England Transcendentalists in the United States. The movement was essentially literary rather than scientific, but one of high distinction, whose significance has not been fully realised even yet.

On the purely occult front, after the seventeenth century, little happened on the surface, but there was a corresponding growth of a number of secret or semi-secret organisations, centering around various forms of freemasonry, although most freemasonry today appears to be, in the main, a friendly society structured around various occult ritual forms and philosophies that most of its members no longer understand.

In fact secret societies became something of a vogue. Some of these were quite superficial; others were religious, scientific and literary discussion groups with ritualistic trimmings. At the disreputable end of the scale were catch penny organisations dispensing grand sounding initiations, at a price, or circles of degenerates who gave piquancy to their deviant practices with the fashionable trimmings of secret rituals of a blasphemous or salacious nature. One example of such was the notorious Hellfire Club. Other secret societies were a cloak for political activities and in particular the Jacobite cause of restoring the Stuart monarchy.

There were however a number of genuine attempts to reconstitute an equivalent of the ancient mystery religions, each of which tended to form about the nucleus of a particularly strong, or inspired, personality.

One such was Louis Claude de St. Martin, who founded the Martinist Order, branches of which still exist. He was sympathetic to Christian belief, although this did not prevent his books being placed upon the Papal Index, and he looked toward every human being developing their innate spiritual quality with the eventual goal of attaining an ideal society. He in turn had been an initiate of a form of masonry developed by Martines de Pasqually, who founded the Rite of Elect Cohens in 1754. This had seven grades of initiation leading to that of Rose Croix, and was based on a view of a long evolutionary journey of man, partly as recorded in the Old Testament, but going back long before Genesis.

Another important esoteric group of the times was the Illuminati, founded in 1776 by Adam Weishampt, a professor of law at the University of Ingolstadt. Whilst this never grew to large numbers it exerted considerable intellectual influence. It defended liberal ideas against the conservative ecclesiastical approach to university education, and drew much of its inspiration from the ancient Pythagorean tradition and the Eleusinian Mysteries of ancient Greece. It greatly influenced Goethe, who is an important transitional figure in upholding traditional spiritual values in the face of an increasingly materialistic and reductionist scientific method.

The composer Mozart was a member of a masonic brotherhood of the times and this is demonstrated in his opera *The Magic Flute*. This form of masonry had a certain ancient Egyptian flavour, and this tradition occurs also in the work of a colourful personality Count Allesandro Cagliostro, who founded the Egyptian Rite of Freemasonry. Although accused of charlatanry and deception, he established a strong following for some time in the aristocratic circles of Europe with a display of healing, visionary and prophetic powers. He ended his life as a prisoner of the Inquisition, in 1795, having fallen from favour in the French court and having been lured to Rome, sentenced to life imprisonment for heresy.

Another charismatic figure of the time was the Comte de St. Germain who, if all that is said of him is true, was a living embodiment of the tradition of the wonder working adept of secret arts. He is said to have spoken eleven languages, played several musical instruments, composed music including an opera, painted strangely luminous pictures, removed flaws from gems, had a profound historical knowledge, the gift of prophecy, and also the secret of the elixir of life, for there are reports of his being active, under various aliases, from 1710 to 1822!

There are also two religious movements with strong occult overtones that commenced in the 18th century. One of these is that of Karl von Eckartshausen who wrote a number of books based on an esoteric approach to science and religion, including the tradition of a secret school of spiritually advanced human beings, or adepts. The best known of these works is *The Cloud Upon the Sanctuary*. The other important religious innovator was Emanuel Swedenborg, a man of many accomplishments. Trained as a mining engineer, and metallurgist he was also proficient in astronomy, physics, zoology, anatomy, finance, economics, classics and theology. As an inventor he made sketches for flying machines, submarines, machine guns and various pumps. He was raised to the Swedish nobility because of his abilities but gave up a successful career to devote himself to the promulgation of psychic visions which he had experienced since a child. Some of his clairvoyant powers were investigated and pronounced genuine by the philosopher Immanuel Kant. A Swedenborgian Church was eventually established on his voluminous writings, which still exists, and profoundly influenced the early William Blake.

On the more scientific approach to occult phenomena considerable attention was attracted by Dr Anton Mesmer of the University of Vienna who effected cures for nervous diseases by the use of magnetic plates. He practised with enormous success and was offered

a considerable fortune by the King of France if he would found a
school to teach his methods. His method was based upon the use of
a circular 'magnetised' tub and the theory of 'animal magnetism' as a
curative force. However, committees of established medical practi-
tioners declared in 1784 that, having investigated his claims, there
was no evidence for such a force.

In the same year the Marquis de Puysegur began to produce similar
effects without the use of a magnetic tub. He used a tree instead. But
from his work there developed the condition known as 'somnam-
bulism' or deep hypnotic trance. In 1813 the Abbé Faria in his
investigations confirmed that it was the imagination that played a key
role in this kind of phenomena, not artificial aids. And in 1841–5 the
British scientist Baird claimed to have proved the possibility of
producing all the phenomena of 'animal magnetism' simply by the
use of suggestion. This marked the end of 'mesmerism' and the
beginning of 'hypnotism', which was used occasionally to produce
anaesthesia in surgery until the discovery of chloroform in the late
1840's.

However, it is arguable that dismissing 'animal magnetism' as 'all
imagination' was, in some respects a classic case of throwing out the
baby with the magnetic bath water, and in other respects a staggering
blindness at regarding the human imagination as something of little
account. The fallacy of this was realised by the poet Samuel Taylor
Coleridge, who combined a brilliant intellect and artistic gift with a
close aquaintance with the effects of opium. His resulting insights
into the powers, depths and heights of the human mind brought
about his theory of the imagination as a creative power when
properly used and not confused with mere fantasy. His tragic
addiction prevented him from writing a consistent systematic
account of his insights, although this has in large part been done in
latter years by the analysis of all his writings by Owen Barfield, in his
monumental work *What Coleridge Thought*.

The stage was, however, being set for the resurgence of truth and
of these powerful forces that both religious and scientific orthodoxy
had for more than two hundred years been striving to deny.

10 THE PAST ONE HUNDRED AND FIFTY YEARS

The resurgence of the occult

The occult knocked heavily at the door, so to speak, on 31st March 1848, with the strange rapping noises at the home of the Fox sisters, in Hydesville, New York state. They interpreted these as signals which eventually led to the discovery of the bones of a murdered man in the cellar. Thus was the modern Spiritualist movement born. These early manifestations of what appeared to be communication between the living and the dead were soon eclipsed by remarkable phenomena produced by professional mediums which included physical levitation, appearance of phantoms, and spirit photography.

From America the movement spread to Europe with a tremendous craze for table turning, table tapping, automatic writing and similar activities for attempting to contact the departed. The movement included Queen Victoria and attracted the attention of a number of prominent scientists and literati, including Conan Doyle, the creator of that very logical fictional detective, Sherlock Holmes, and Sir William Crookes, the eminent physicist and a President of the Royal Society.

The Society for Psychical Research was brought into being largely in response to this outbreak of psychic phenomena, with the purpose of investigating it strictly in accordance with the tenets of materialist scientific discipline. It still exists and holds a mass of attested documentation. The Spiritualist movement also continues to exist, in considerable strength, largely as a church, offering evidence for survival through approved mediums and clairvoyants.

There was always from the first, and there still remains, considerable controversy as to the genuineness of the recorded phenomena, and also whether any messages received could be taken at face value. That is, whether they were actual communications from the deceased or simply subconscious memories on the part of the sitters, perhaps feeding in telepathically to the medium.

Similarly some of the more spectacular phenomena of levitation, teleportation, phantom forms, met with accusations, some of them well founded, of cheating. And some sceptical professional illusionists, such as Harry Houdini, claimed to be able to duplicate the phenomena by perfectly natural means. These arguments carry on right into the present day with the claims surrounding popular figures such as the fork bending Uri Geller.

For better or for worse, the Spiritualist movement has not developed a comprehensive spiritual philosophy, which causes some of its detractors to say it would be better named 'spiritist', for it begins and ends with, for the most part, relatively trivial personal spirit messages. However, there has been a parallel development of occult philosophical and practical teachings that have been produced by similar psychical means.

The most influential of such is undoubtedly H.P. Blavatsky, a Russian born woman who showed remarkable psychic gifts even as a small child which quite terrified her Russian Orthodox relatives. Following an early and disastrous marriage she spent most of her early womanhood travelling in Europe and the East and came to prominence in 1875 in New York with the publication of a monumental work entitled *Isis Unveiled* which threw down the gauntlet to religious and scientific orthodoxy with claims for the validity of the existence of the inner worlds behind material appearances. Under the banner of forming a universal brotherhood of those who could see the one truth behind all religions, she founded the Theosophical Society, which has had a profound influence on much modern occult thought.

Although capable of producing spiritualist messages and psychic phenomena she did not endorse the claims of spiritualists that they were in fact communicating with the departed. She herself claimed to have made contact with a body of superior beings who were world teachers, a large part of whose teaching she published in *The Secret Doctrine* in 1888.

The teaching is a vast cosmology giving a history of the universe, inner and outer, based on some hitherto unknown Eastern texts known only to the occult masters or 'mahatmas' with whom she was in clairvoyant contact. These books remain available for any interested reader to assess and the Theosophical Society became largely an organisation for publicising and promulgating these teachings. In this it received considerable impetus through the conversion of the pioneering feminist, trade unionist, and free thinker, Annie Besant who gave her very considerable energy and talents to the cause.

The influence of this teaching has been far reaching and pervasive. Most adherents of esoteric thought today owe many of their assumptions to Madame Blavatsky or her mahatmas. This applies even to those who purport to eschew oriental influence in their beliefs. There have also been diverse developments of those claiming to carry on the tradition of teaching, either inside or outside the Theosophical Society, with continuing contacts with the Masters.

One of the most influential of these is Alice Bailey, who produced a large number of books in her life, by clairaudient or intuitive means. These develop the material set out in Blavatsky's *Secret Doctrine*, of which the first major one was *A Treatise on Cosmic Fire* published in 1925 and followed up inter alia with *A Treatise on White Magic* and a five volume *Treatise on the Seven Rays* to name but the major works. They do not make for easy reading but nonetheless they have formed the basis of a worldwide movement based on the ideals of universal brotherhood and an analysis in some detail of the "nuts and bolts" of the seven planes behind and beyond the physical plane.

Another major influence on modern esoteric thought are the teachings of Rudolf Steiner, the founder of Anthroposophy, which is largely based upon the spiritual scientific insights of Goethe, although with considerable additions that make this particular occult movement notable for its practical concerns with education, agriculture, holistic medicine, art, science, and technology. Steiner's general worldview is expressed in *Occult Science: an outline*, first published in 1913 although there is a considerable corpus of works, including many lectures on specific topics.

Gurdjieff should also be mentioned as an important occult figure of the modern epoch, whose teachings have largely been published and developed by his followers P.D. Ouspensky, Maurice Nicoll or Rodney Collin. The writer Kathleen Mansfield was also much influenced by him. The general aim of this teaching, as indeed with any of the other esoteric presentations mentioned, is to awaken people to a different level of consciousness. There are, of course, various means whereby this can be done, hence the diversity of organisations and teachers.

One important organisation that had a relatively short life yet which has exercised considerable and growing influence was the somewhat colourfully named Hermetic Order of the Golden Dawn, which developed from the wholly western Rosicrucian and Masonic traditions. It also, like Madame Blavatsky, derived its authority from Masters or 'Secret Chiefs' although its outer driving force was S.L. MacGregor Mathers, who put together most of the rituals and knowledge papers from his personal researches at the British Museum.

The Order attracted a number of celebrated adherents of whom the one most remembered by posterity is the poet W.B. Yeats. It is most notable, however, for the continuing influence that it has exercised over the subsequent century, largely through the teaching and works of a succeeding generation of those who had been its members, or members of its off-shoots. Of these we could name A.E. Waite, Aleister Crowley, Israel Regardie, Paul Case, and Dion Fortune, although there were a number of others less well known because they did not venture into print, but who were nonetheless influential teachers.

Of those we have listed A.E. Waite was the most scholarly and spiritually inclined and later went on to form a group of his own on more mystical lines than the strongly magically oriented Golden Dawn tradition. He translated a number of important works into English, including the French occultist Eliphas Levi, and wrote a considerable body of work on various occult topics, from alchemy to the Holy Grail tradition. Unfortunately his style is heavily Edwardian largely because he was very sensitive to the demi-monde reputation of occult studies and seemed to feel that a pomposity of style would add a certain degree of respectability. However, he was a reasonably accurate scholar and did much to preserve neglected tradition and make it more accessible. Ironically his greatest impact has been in an area which he claimed not to take too seriously, the design of Tarot cards. A set that he designed, with the aid of the artist Pamela Coleman-Smith, and published in 1910, has become perhaps the most popular of modern packs and has also influenced a number of other new designs.

Aleister Crowley was a very different personality, an *enfant terrible* of the occultism of his day. His penchant for outrageous behaviour and self advertisement led him to become the first victim of a modern press campaign of vilification when he was dubbed "the wickedest man in the world" by Horatio Bottomley's *John Bull*. Whilst Crowley was probably more flattered than disturbed by such attention, his capacity for evil was very small beer by most political and criminological or even commercial standards, and was largely in the sphere of sexual excesses and drug abuse within his own private circle of influence. Although his initial scientific attitude to altered states of consciousness, which led him to psychological experimentation upon himself and others by such methods, has earned him a certain qualified respect, he is not a good example for any inexperienced student to follow. He fished in some deep and quite dangerous occult waters and is not above making quite misleading statements as a private joke against his readers. For the discerning reader, however, his works can still prove informative and even entertaining.

Israel Regardie's name is closely associated with the Golden Dawn first through a number of books he wrote as a young man whilst under its influence, and subsequently because he took it upon himself, when the Order was largely defunct, to preserve its teaching for a wider audience by publishing its rituals and knowledge papers. Thus, for the benefit of succeeding generations, a complete and workable practical system is laid before the public, as a quarry for private work and investigation.

Paul Case and Dion Fortune, each in their way, preserved the Golden Dawn tradition in a less public way by forming their own esoteric groups, largely based upon its traditions. Paul Case in America, where he founded the Builders of the Adytum, the teaching of which is largely concentrated upon the Tarot. Dion Fortune in England, whose Society of the Inner Light, since its foundation in the early 1920's has been the training ground for a number of well known occult writers, including W.E. Butler, Gareth Knight, and Dolores Ashcroft-Nowicki, to say nothing of individual teachers who have been of considerable influence without launching into print.

The United States of America has also produced a number of organisations devoted to the Western esoteric tradition besides that of Paul Case. Perhaps the one that is foremost in the public eye through its national advertising is AMORC, a Rosicrucian organisation with impressive headquarters at San José in California, and at other places in the world, such as the Rosicrucian Centre in Paris, with modern shop, meeting halls and even radio studio.

Perhaps less well known but nonetheless worthy of note is the Rosicrucian Fellowship, founded by Max Heindel, author of a classic popular occult textbook *The Rosicrucian Cosmo-Conception*.

The recent publications of Melita Denning and Osborne Philips, under the title of *The Magical Philosophy* have also revealed the teachings of an American magical fraternity, the Order of the Sacred Word, founded in 1897.

And whilst it is plainly impracticable to try to list every group, even of a major nature, mention should be made of Manley Palmer Hall, founder of the Philosophical Research Society, whose *Secret Teachings of All Ages* is an encyclopaedic occult text and reference book based on sympathetic and accurate scholarship.

Whilst most of these groups had their beginnings in the pre-war years, or even earlier, there has been a considerable resurgence of interest in occult theory and practice particularly since the 1960's.

During this time the main stream of Western tradition has been strengthened by the works of W.G. Gray, whose four-fold magical circle, based on age old universal principles, but expounded in a logical and practical way in *Magical Ritual Methods* and later books, has influenced a new generation of students and teachers. And a fresh approach to the Golden Dawn system of symbolism has been developed by Edwin Steinbrecher in his book *The Guide Meditation* and organisation, the DOME Foundation.

A major trend in this period has been the growth of neo-pagan interest. This ranges from ecological concerns on a world wide basis, through nature mysticism, to shamanism, folk traditions, and interest in ancient sites. The scholarly foundations to this trend were laid principally by Dr Margaret Murray in *The Witch Cult in Western Europe* and *The God of the Witches* and in a more speculative vein by the famous *The White Goddess* by Robert Graves.

At a more popular level was the work of G.B. Gardner who instituted a number of practising pagan groups, assisted by books such as *The Meaning of Witchcraft* which has led to a number of similar works following his lead. There is a certain amount of doubt as to the wisdom of using the word 'witchcraft' in this manner, partly because of unfortunate connotations in the past, but despite the occasional lurid journalistic article rising to the bait, the move-ment is generally respectable enough. There is a certain amount of debate as to how much Gerald Gardner's system is genuinely traditional, and how much of his own making, but it certainly seems good enough to satisfy a fair number of adherents.

The existence of a group of people hungry for this kind of approach is vouched for by the continuing success of *Quest* magazine, edited by Marian Green, which caters to a young readership attracted to traditional nature magic and lore. It has survived for over 20 years, (remarkable longevity for a small privately published and produced magazine) and forms the focus for a number of local 'Green Circle' groups of enquirers.

There has also been a considerable interest in more exotic native traditions which received a considerable impetus from the books of Carlos Castaneda commencing with *The Teachings of Don Juan*, a Pueblo Indian, in 1968 and going on to develop the theme in later books that certainly stretch the imagination.

However, a broader approach to native folk traditions has been developed by, for example, Bob Stewart, a musician turned writer, who has investigated the powerful imagery of folksong to draw occult conclusions that are of seminal importance for future research, in a number of books of which *The UnderWorld Initiation* is perhaps the most important. He has also gone on to embrace the magical tradition in the Arthurian legends through a number of books and conferences on the figure of Merlin. Allied to this trend are the books of Caitlin and John Matthews, covering aspects of the Grail tradition, and including a comprehensive two volume treatment of both Native and Hermetic strands of Western occultism in *The Western Way*.

Perhaps of more popular appeal has been the increasing interest in the pioneering work of Alfred Watkins who first proposed the concept of 'ley-lines' early in the century. Recent years have seen his work rescued from obscurity and developed in a way that he could hardly have imagined. In part this has embraced the scientific appraisal of megalithic sites as ancient astronomical observatories, and also the detection with pendulum or dowsing rod or other means of lines of psychic force around or connecting various sites. Allied to this are concepts of sacred geometry that also link in to Gothic and Renaissance architecture.

Generally speaking there has indeed been a resurgence of interest in all branches of occult study, whether it be based on traditions of East or West, of the intellectual Hermetic approach, or the search for mystical personal enlightenment, or the turning to native traditions in the love and concern for nature. Some of the forms of expression of this interest could perhaps have been better expressed, but together they indicate a hunger for truths that will not go away, or human needs that are plainly not being catered for by current scientific, religious or political visions.

PART TWO
An Occult Glossary with recommended reading

ALCHEMY came to us via the Arabs, as its prefix 'al' implies, although originating perhaps in ancient Egypt, known once as *Khem*. There is also evidence for a Chinese origin, perhaps independently. Writers on the history of science generally regard it as a primitive form of chemistry, and to a large extent, in its laboratory experiments, it certainly was. A number of elements and important components were first isolated by alchemists at a time when chemistry and alchemy went hand in hand.

The psychologist Jung has, however, investigated a whole new approach to the subject. He sees it as a 'projection' of the alchemist's inner desires, his soul or psychological processes, onto a physical experiment. Thus in psychological terms the distillation process of the first solution of the mysterious 'prima materia' or First Matter, is the stirring of the 'unconscious' into some kind of integrating or spiritual activity.

Alchemical symbols of Salt, Mercury and Sulphur

In this Jung follows a lead given by a pioneering work of Mrs. Atwood, *A Suggestive Enquiry into the Hermetic Mystery*. Jung's researches into the subject have unearthed a number of interesting alchemical diagrams and theories, whether one wishes to take his psychological interpretations at face value or not (e.g. *Psychology and Alchemy, Mysterium Coniunctionis, Alchemical Studies*, etc.).

Another modern writer, Titus Burkhardt (in *Alchemy*) interprets the alchemical process as a psycho/spiritual one, seeing the stages of the process exemplified by the traditional symbols for the metals. The whole process is one involving consciousness, and the action of positive and negative principles upon it. These are symbolised by Mercury, Sulphur and Salt respectively.

From a base state represented by Lead the reflective principle of consciousness is raised up to a pure reflective state of Silver. The next stage begins with the dawning of a spiritual radiating principle in consciousness which gradually rises to a position of dominance and subsequently to full control, a condition symbolised by Gold.

Alchemical terms are very complex and confusing when one reads original alchemical texts. The process is often described by colours: a black solution (nigredo) proceeding through greening (viriditas) to a white colour (albedo), from whence comes a range of all the colours in quick succession (cauda pavonis or peacock's tail) and a reddening to pure gold.

It should be said that there is rare and isolated (though well testified) evidence of actual gold having been made. Those who wish to try a practical 'hands on' approach, commencing with the preparation of herbal elixirs would do best to consult *The Alchemists Handbook* by Frater Albertus which is a modern manual for practical laboratory alchemy.

ANTHROPOSOPHY is an approach to occultism associated with Rudolf Steiner (1861–1925) that is also often called Spiritual Science. The name derives from the Greek *anthropos* – man, and *sophia* – wisdom, and is so called because it is a human based approach to scientific and philosophical questions. Indeed the Anthroposophical Society and its associated individuals and organisations have arguably done more than most to express occult principles in physical terms, with their farms, schools, and scientific pursuits, including medicine.

Most of the literature of the movement is in German in the original but has been translated in a host of books and pamphlets. Much of the fundamental inspiration comes from the genius of Goethe (1749–1832), of whose work Rudolf Steiner made a profound study.

However, as a clairvoyant of an apparently cosmic range of perception, Steiner built a considerable edifice of teaching upon this base.

His basic book is *Knowledge of the Higher Worlds*, describing how to attain it; with *Occult Science; an outline* as a general description of the supersensible worlds as descried by him. A good general introduction to Steiner's thought is to be found in *Rudolf Steiner's Vision of Love* by Bernard Nesfield-Cookson.

There are also some distinguished and thought provoking books by other Anthroposophists on specific areas of research of which the following might make a reasonable short list.

The Plant Between Sun and Earth by George Adams and Olive Whicher, a profusely illustrated work guiding the reader through the study of plant forms to an appreciation of the dynamics of the spiritual worlds.

Encounters with the Infinite by Heidi Keller-von Asten, a work book of projective geometry, a branch of mathematics that needs no prior mathematical knowledge but can lead to an expansion of consciousness through the drawing of various beautiful mathematical forms. A more theoretical approach is to be found in *Projective Geometry* by Olive Whicher, again copiously and imaginatively illustrated.

Man or Matter by Ernst Lehrs, an account of a way of extending the bounds of scientific understanding by an application of the principles of Goethe to modern science. Similarly *The Nature of Substance* by Rudolf Hauschka.

Astronomy and the Imagination by Norman Davidson is a new, and yet in another sense very old, approach to man's experience of the stars based on the importance of naked eye astronomy and the imaginative faculty of man.

This imaginative faculty and its fundamental importance is developed as a coherent philosophy in *What Coleridge Thought*, by Owen Barfield, who reconstructs it from the scattered writings of the poet/philosopher S.T. Coleridge. Barfield is also author of an important philosophical treatise in his own right called *Saving the Appearances* which encapsulates this line of thought.

There are more books that one could mention of a specialist nature on colour and art and movement, education and drama, organic farming and holistic medicine, for example, following through the principles of Spiritual Science in various areas of life. However these are perhaps best personally investigated by a visit to the Rudolf Steiner Centre in London.

ARTHURIAN LEGEND, like all legend and mythology, is important
to practical occultism because it is the language of the deeper levels of
consciousness. What dreams are to individuals, myths and legends
are to a race or nation, or even all mankind.

The legends of King Arthur and his Knights of the Round Table
are particularly important in that they have an almost universal
appeal, although they originated for the most part in the British
Isles.

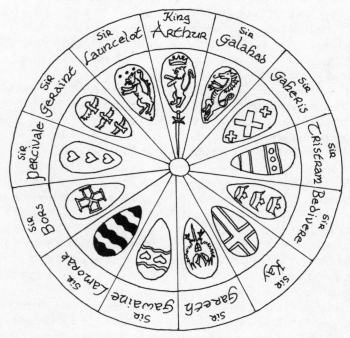

A version of King Arthur's Round Table

The ideal of an order of chivalry devoted to bringing justice and
good rule to the land is a part of it, as also the individual heroism of
the various knights, and their relationships with their ladies, who
vary from great powerful queens and enchantresses to idyllically
beautiful damsels in distress. Magic plays an important part in the
form of Merlin, who is no mere enchanter, but a man conscious of
the destiny of nations and of the great sweep of affairs of the world.

The Holy Grail also plays a part in all of this, at many levels of being, from a miraculous underworld cauldron that can rejuvenate warriors or give inspiration, to a mystical vision of the highest and most sublime sanctity. Thus there is a complete run through of human consciousness, from depths to the heights, and extremely wide ranging too. Some equate the Round Table with the circle of the Zodiac and the knights and ladies with great cosmic figures. Others trace the origins of the legends to forgotten history of fabled continents such as lost Atlantis. It is also possible to seek out physical sites in the British Isles and France with Arthurian associations, adding an element of pilgrimage to the practical study.

For English readers the core text is *Le Morte d'Arthur* of Sir Thomas Malory, one of the first books to be printed in England, by Thomas Caxton in 1485. It is still available in paperback. Malory, a knight in the Wars of the Roses, made his collection and translation from various sources when he was imprisoned, and it is from him that we get the tradition of knights jousting in plate armour and travelling in a scene of Norman type castles. Most of us come to the stories via redactions for children, which is how all good myths and legends are preserved, if in slightly bowdlerised fashion.

Other principle texts available in paperback include the anonymous *The Quest of the Holy Grail, The High History of the Holy Grail, Gawain and the Green Knight* and *The Death of King Arthur, Arthurian Chronicles* by Wace and Layamon, *History of the Kings of Britain* by Geoffrey of Monmouth, *Tristan* by Gottfried von Strassburg, *The Romance of Tristan* by Beroul, *Arthurian Romances* by Chretien de Troyes, *Lais* of Marie de France and the old Welsh tales in *The Mabinogion*. Those who are really keen however will do with nothing less than the three volume *The Works of Sir Thomas Malory* edited by Eugene Vinaver from the Winchester Manuscript discovered as late as 1934.

There are also some excellent and informative books about the Arthurian legends, characters and sites, from a historical and occult point of view. First we should mention *The Secret Tradition in Arthurian Legend* by Gareth Knight as a general comprehensive occult coverage, and the figure of Merlin is given detailed treatment by R.J. Stewart in *The Mystic Life of Merlin* and *The Prophecies of Merlin*. The Holy Grail is well covered by John Matthews and Marian Green in *The Grail Seeker's Companion* and John Matthews has also edited a collection of essays by various contributors called *At the Table of the Grail*. The Mabinogion stories are also well elucidated by Caitlin Matthews in *Mabon and the Mysteries of Britain*.

More general introductory books that can be recommended are *The Quest for Arthur's Britain*, a sound account of the history and the literature and legend; *King Arthur and the Grail* by Richard Cavendish; and *The Arthurian Legends*, an illustrated anthology by Richard Barber.

The Arthurian legends have also attracted the attention of poets and novelists, *The Idylls of the King* by Tennyson are Victorian poetic classics, and *Arthurian Poems* by Charles Williams, modern ones. *The Once and Future King* by T.H. White has achieved enormous popularity, and *The Mists of Avalon* by Marion Bradley also has a sizable following. Mary Stewart has written a series of novels based on Merlin, *The Crystal Cave, The Hollow Hills, The Last Enchantment*, and *The Wicked Day*, and Rosemary Sutcliffe has covered the Holy Grail in *The Light Beyond the Forest* and the last days in *The Road to Camlan*. A novel based on Arthur's queen is *Guinevere Evermore* by Sharon Newman, and Parke Godwin has written a trilogy of a Dark Age historical Arthur in *Firelord, Beloved Exile*, and *The Last Rainbow*, Excellent re-telling of the tales for children, which are also worthwhile for adults, can be found in *The Sword and the Circle* by Rosemary Sutcliffe and *King Arthur and his Knights* by A. Mockler.

ASTRAL PROJECTION is the experience of being conscious of oneself as a coherent personality outside one's physical body. Many who have undergone it assess it as personal evidence of the survival of bodily death. The principle first-hand account of a series of such experiences is by Sylvan Muldoon, assisted by psychical researcher Hereward Carrington. It is notable that Sylvan Muldoon was seldom in the best of health and also that one projection was caused through shock by a fallen power cable! Following the publication of their book, *The Projection of the Astral Body*, they were able to follow it up with accounts by members of the public who had written to them with similar experiences.

Other experiential and methodological books include, *Astral Projection* by Yram, (translated from the French), *Astral Projection* by Oliver Fox and *The Art and Practice of Astral Projection* by Ophiel.

The methods used vary from training oneself to dissociate consciousness in sleep when dreaming, to complex visualisation of oneself as a 'body' outside one's physical body and then transferring

The soul in the form of a bird hovering over the mummy

The 'Astral Body' in ancient Egypt

consciousness. It is not an easy feat unless one has a particular 'gift' for it. The more recent *Journeys Out of the Body* by the American businessman Robert Monroe, is particularly interesting in that Monroe had no occult interest or inclinations at all, but suddenly found it happening to him. At first he thought he might be going mad and indeed did seek psychiatric help, but received little aid or comprehension.

His experiences confirm various types of projection. One form is close to the physical world with the ability to pass through solid objects and to move at great speed. Others are in being projected to other kinds of worlds, even with a different technology. Some experiences are evidently symbolic in character.

Emotion seems to play an important role in this level of experience and feelings of dislike can cause quite violent upsets and confrontations on 'the astral'. There is also a silver thread or cord found linking the physical and projected bodies, and it is felt that this is the thread of vitality which, if it were broken, would result in death. It is thought by some to be referred to in the Bible in the phrase "if ever the silver cord be loosed or the golden bowl [*the projected aura*] be broken."

ASTROLOGY as a serious pursuit suffers drastically from its popularity. The astrological columns in the popular press are no more than entertainment journalism for it is plainly unlikely that a short paragraph on each 'Sun sign' should be able to predict events for one twelfth of the population.

The twelve divisions used by astrological journalists are the sign in the heavens that the Sun happened to appear in at the date of birth. If one knows one's birthday one knows one's Sun sign, and important though the position of the Sun may be in astrology proper, it is but one facet among a great number of others.

An astrological horoscope is a chart of the sky as seen from the place on the surface of the Earth at the moment of birth. There are thus, besides these two factors of accurate place and time, the positions of the Sun, the Moon and the planets. These are calculated in relation to the background of fixed stars (the Zodiac) against which they appear, their position above or below the horizon, (their House), and the angles they may make one with another (their Aspects).

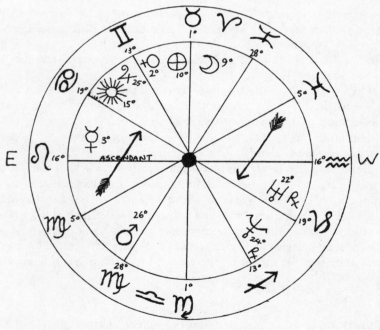

An Astrological Chart

Having mounted such a chart, which calls for a fair degree of astronomical knowledge and arithmetical ability, the task remains of interpreting it. Although sceptics say that this means that all babies born in the same maternity hospital at the same time are stamped with the same character, those who have had their horoscopes drawn up and interpreted often find it a helpful guide.

There are various extensions from the basic Natal chart. The planetary and other positions can be extended forward in time with the idea of making predictions of future influences, trends or events. Also astrological charts can be made of nations for a political interpretation (Mundane Astrology), or for the birth of an idea (Horary Astrology).

Jeff Mayo's popular book *Teach Yourself Astrology* is a good exposition by an intelligent practitioner for anyone new to the subject, and the literature of the subject is, in fact, vast. Alternatively *The Modern Textbook of Astrology* by Margaret Hone also provides a very sound foundation to serious study.

The AURA is the field of radiation about every living being; humans, animals, trees and plants, and indeed large conglomerates of such, from woods and hills to houses, villages and towns. The feeling of a sense of 'atmosphere' about a place or person is a part of it, which most people can sense, demonstrating that psychism is a perfectly natural and common means of perception.

However, some people by natural gift or training may see it as actual colours in the air, so to speak. Again most people can see this to some extent if they only try. Try looking at a tree from a distance, slightly defocussing your eyes. Or else try moving your open hands together and apart against a dark background. You may see lines of misty light joining the finger ends between your two hands.

At a more physical level attempts have been made to produce special light filters, or aura goggles, for such observation. This approach was associated with Dr W.J. Kilner, of St. Thomas Hospital, London, who experimented with it as a diagnostic technique in the 1920's and his book *The Human Aura* remains a classic text. When a person is run down their aura looks correspondingly lack-lustre in whole or in part.

At another level a person's moods and emotions are shown forth by different colours in the aura that are apparent to clairvoyant perception. An interesting treatment of this topic, with colour illustrations, is *Thought Forms* by A. Besant and C.W. Leadbeater.

The aura also has power points within it, called *chakras*, and upon this subject much practical and theoretical occultism is based, whether in regard to the human aura or the wider field of geomantic currents or force fields in the landscape, where such centres are likely to be sacred sites, natural features, or centres of population.

A good modern study of the human aura in general is *The Raiment of Light* by David Tansley.

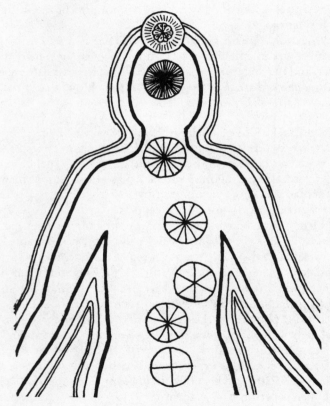

Chakras in the Human Aura

CHAKRAS are key points in the human aura. There are indeed very many of them, some accounts listing seventy or more. However, it is usually only the seven or so principle ones that are emphasised as important for general practical work, those that align more or less with the spinal column.

These are to be found in the crown of the head or a little above it; at the brow, sometimes called the 'third eye'; at the throat; the heart; the solar plexus; the spleen; the genital area; the base of the spine.

The chakras form the basis of a considerable amount of occult theory and practice, and in many and various ways. They are, for instance, visualised in association with breathing exercises and physical postures in the different forms of yoga, as a means of gaining control over the mind and body, inwardly and outwardly.

Again, in the extensive works of Alice Bailey, the chakras and their correspondence at various levels of awareness, from sub-atomic particles to the cosmic consciousness of planetary and stellar beings, form a ground base for a complete system of teaching with far reaching ramifications.

CLAIRVOYANCE comes in many forms and degrees. The most popular is probably that of crystal-gazing, though in fact the true clairvoyant can utilise any object which acts as a focus for concentration. In parts of the world where crystals are hard to come by, a pool of ink in the palm of the hand may be used. Other methods may be seeing 'pictures in the fire', or the contemplation of the tea-leaves in a cup.

It might be called a very light form of self-hypnosis, or trance; it is the inducing of a kind of dreaminess, or waking day-dream. Whilst, for most of us, such a process would simply produce subjective phantasies, the gifted clairvoyant can pick up memories, feelings or psychic conditions.

This is indeed the strength and weakness of clairvoyance, for it may well be picking up the subjective phantasies of the person consulting the clairvoyant. This would be the more so if this person were thinking and feeling very strongly about some problem.

Similarly, those who consult clairvoyants for messages from recently deceased relatives have usually been dwelling upon these relatives in their grief so the clairvoyant may well pick up a 'thought form' rather than a real communication. Seemingly good evidence for survival after death may thus be presented by the clairvoyant when all that is being proved is an ability for mental telepathy.

A good and experienced clairvoyant should know when this kind of thing is happening. But whilst some clairvoyants are particularly gifted and wise in the use of their gifts there are many who are not. It is also a faculty that tends to come and go in a somewhat unpredictable fashion so that even good clairvoyants have their 'off' days. This is one reason why professional clairvoyance can lead to abuses where the clairvoyant is expected to give results, for a fee, at a specific date and time. Those good enough and honest enough will admit to it when their powers temporarily wane; others less gifted or ethical may be tempted to fake results.

An excellent introduction to the subject by a responsible and experienced master of the art is *How To Develop Clairvoyance* by W.E. Butler.

CRYSTALS have attracted increasing attention in the last few years, although there has always been a deep occult interest in them that was the preserve of a few, and there are also a number of popular legends and stories about the mysterious power of precious stones, for good or for evil.

Ever since quartz crystals were thought to be petrified ice by the miners who discovered them, up until the comparatively recent advances in scientific understanding of atomic and molecular structure of crystalline forms, they have stimulated man's imagination because they are naturally occurring forms that give the appearance of intelligent design in beautiful geometric forms.

Natural crystal forms

They are considered to be accumulators and processing agents of psychic force in much the same way that some of them, particularly the quartzes, are able to change mechanical energy into electrical energy or light energy, which enables them to be utilised in modern electronic circuitry, from the now somewhat primitive 'crystal set' of early radio, to the silicon chip of modern high technology.

Silica is one of the most common substances on the face of the Earth, it is the basis of sand for example, and the atoms of quartz crystals are made up of atoms of silicon and oxygen arranged in tetrahedra, or four sided pyramids, a form that excited the mystical interest of the ancient sages, as one of the Platonic Solids.

A number of books have appeared on the market in response to the growth of interest in crystals, and their quality is variable. However a good introduction is to be found in the books of Ra Bonewitz, who is a trained mineralogist as well as appreciative of their occult properties. These are *Cosmic Crystals* and *The Cosmic Crystal Spiral*.

Crystal gazing is a rather specialised technique of clairvoyance of considerable antiquity, usually involving the use of a crystal ball to focus attention. For purists this ball would be made of quartz crystal, and thus of considerable expense. Others are content with glass, which is much cheaper, (or should be). Certainly quartz has an inner regular tetrahedal atomic structure of its own, whereas glass has no inner structure at all, being technically merely a super-cooled liquid, which is why medieval glass windows are thicker at the bottom than the top because they continue to flow, albeit very slowly. However, others claim that this type of clairvoyance can equally well be done with any similar type of shiny surface, such as a pool of ink in the palm of the hand, or – less messy – a black tile or bottle containing black liquid, John Melville's *Crystal Gazing and Clairvoyance* is a handy introduction to the technique.

DIVINATION is related to clairvoyance which is used, albeit unconsciously, in most good divination. More emphasis is placed on the mechanics of the operation and these are likely to take one of several forms:

a) **cartomancy**, or card reading, either with ordinary playing cards, or with the Tarot (q.v.);
b) the **I Ching**, an ancient Chinese system (q.v.);
c) **geomancy** (q.v.) a method using marks made in sand.

In olden times there was a host of other 'omancies' ranging from foretelling the future from the flight of birds to examining the entrails of slaughtered animals.

The rationale for the practice has received some support from Jung in his foreword to Wilhelm's translation of the *I Ching* and in his

work *Synchronicity – An Acausal Connecting Principle*. Briefly, the idea
is that any particular moment in time has its own quality. Therefore
to consult a random pattern of conventional symbols cast at a
particular time and with a particular intention is a means of gauging
the invisible forces at work at that time and in that context.

Whatever the theory, it seems to work for some people and faith in
its working seems to be an important factor. This leads to the
corollary that those who disbelieve are unlikely to receive personal
proof of its efficacy.

An attitude of faith and belief whilst consulting the oracle, coupled
with a healthy and critical scepticism of its results is recommended by
most advocates of the system – blind credulity being no more
encouraged than outright scepticism.

The oracles seem to work best when consulted in an attitude of
respect, as if of a wise old counsellor. For the sceptical it will not
work, and it may lead the credulous a wild and merry dance, playing
on their credulity, by way of teaching them wisdom. As in much of
occultism, one tends to get a combination of what one expects and
what one deserves.

DOWSING is a means of detecting hidden things by psychic methods,
usually through the use of a divining rod or a pendulum.

A divining rod, although traditionally a Y shaped piece of hazel
wood, is often to be found in metallic form, and a popular method
now is simply two pieces of bent wire, one held in each hand so that
they can rotate easily. Cut up coat-hangers seem to be a convenient
source of supply!

The pendulum may similarly be a simple home made device of
almost any relatively heavy object suspended on a piece of cotton or
string, to quite complex professionally produced models, perhaps
containing a hollow compartment in which to place a sample of the
substance being searched for.

Seeking out underground water sources or courses is a traditional
and indeed important use, although it is also possible to detect other
mineral deposits, and those with a gift for it are said to be able to
make quite substantial sums of money assisting prospecting compan-
ies. Some dowsers also claim to be able to do it at a distance, by use
of a map of the area, which certainly is an advantage over difficult
terrain.

Tom Graves is accorded great respect in this field and as a starter

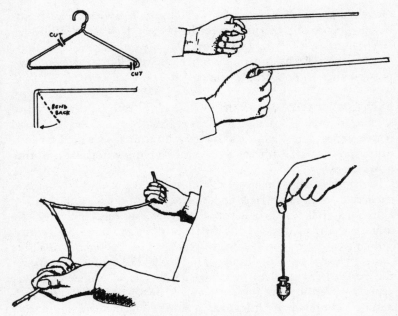

Implements for dowsing

one could hardly do better than consult his much acclaimed clear and comprehensive *The Diviner's Handbook*.

DREAMS are one way in which the occult world may get a message to us. Whilst there are advice columns in popular magazines, and cheap 'dream books', that attempt to interpret the meaning of specific dream images for their readers it is perhaps not so easy or exact a science as that.

By meditation upon particularly vivid dreams an answer to a pressing problem may well come, but every dream is individual to the dreamer, and in the last analysis, it is the dreamer who dreamed the dream who is most likely to be able to fathom out its meaning, even though judicious advice from a friend or other confidant who knows most of the circumstances involved may possibly be of help.

A number of people make a practice of writing down their dreams upon waking as a means of helping them through life, though the practice can be strangely tiring for some. In the 1930's considerable interest developed in recording one's dreams to try to ascertain how often images that arose were not elements of memories of past events but fragments of precognition of the future. This was described in J.W. Dunne's book *An Experiment with Time* and being something of a mathematician and philosopher he went on to develop one possible theory for such phenomena in *The Serial Universe*.

EARTH MYSTERIES constitute a whole range of occult interest and activity that runs parallel to the general concern for ecological responsibility and our duties towards the planet on which we live, other forms of life with which we share it, to say nothing of future generations.

It includes interest in megalithic sites, features of landscape such as the lore and legend of lakes and hills, ley lines, dowsing, mazes and labyrinths, hill figures and other earthworks, and not least the interest in the Goddess in the aspect of the Earth as a living entity.

In ancient mythology the earth goddess Gaia gave birth to all life forms by coupling with Ouranos, the sky god. As a living organism, the Earth, like ourselves, will have an aura, and chakras or power centres within it. This gives a new and inner perspective on such natural phenomena as the solar wind, geomagnetism, the aurora borealis, and so on, to say nothing of sacred sites and the lines of force that run between them.

Earth mysteries inner gateway

Of late, considerable interest has been accorded to American Indian myth and legend, for they seem to have been closer to these natural Earth Mysteries than the conquering races who have since overrun the Americas.

The following is a selection of books that cover various aspects of the Earth Mysteries traditions.

John Michell, *A New View of Atlantis* did much to put Earth Mysteries on the map and covers most of the field.

Paul Devereux and Ian Thomson, *The Ley Guide* is a cheap modern guide to current practice on this subject. The original works by Alfred Watkins are still available and worth study, *The Old Straight Track* and *The Ley Hunter's Manual*.

Nigel Pennick, *The Ancient Science of Geomancy* examines the traditions from various parts of the world, of how primitive man lived in harmony with his natural environment.

Tom Graves, *Needles of Stone Revisited* is a summary of how the land can be healed by dowsing techniques and a renewal of a right attitude toward nature.

Janet and Colin Bord have produced a number of photographically illustrated guides to ancient sites, including *Mysterious Britain, The Secret Country, Ancient Mysteries of Britain, A Guide to Ancient Sites in Britain*.

American Indian traditions are described in *Seven Arrows* by Hyemeyohsts Storm, which has become something of a classic in its field.

ELEMENTALS are a generic name for various forms of consciousness that cannot be classed as human. They range from 'fairies at the bottom of the garden' to great Nature Spirits of natural locations – hill, wood, dale or river. In the higher reaches they become similar to angels or archangels set over countries, nations and races.

The concept of such beings is likely to put a strain upon the credulity of many people today but those who prefer their psychic fauna and flora dressed in scientific terms can approach such ideas via such psychological concepts as 'group minds', 'group souls', or personifications of natural surroundings by projection of aspects of the human personality.

This they may be in part, but the seasoned occultist would go further and credit these beings with an independent and objective existence.

At the fairy end of things we have a close association with folk lore, and K.M. Briggs' novel *Hobberdy Dick* is a fine evocation of the type of life and consciousness that is meant by the term 'elemental' at this level.

Occultists suspect there to be forms of life which are not quite so cosy.

Elementals are traditionally classified by magical writers into four categories, corresponding to the four traditional elements or states of matter. Salamanders for fire (or radiation), sylphs for air (or gas), undines for water (or liquid), gnomes for earth (or the solid state). Much magical training is taken up with the balancing up of the 'elements within', or the subjective counterparts of these physical states.

It is suspected that certain new types of elemental may have come into the Earth's sphere by way of nuclear fission causing a gap in the Earth's psychic envelope. How these make their presence felt is largely unknown. There is also a certain type that feeds off human mass hysteria. With its mechanical beat, flashing lights and high volume certain forms of popular music can generate a crude form of power which is then sucked off to be used in unknown elemental ways.

EXORCISM is the technique of casting out evil spirits.

The churches have begun to take a greater interest in exorcism of late although it remains a very specialised vocation amongst a relatively small number of clergy. This is perhaps just as well.

There is much more to exorcism than simply reciting formulae with bell, book, candle and holy water. It is important to establish all the facts of the case, which may be very involved and difficult to elicit. A genuine case of possession or overshadowing by evil entities must be distinguished from clinical psychological states, whether they be hysteria or schizophrenia – and of course there may be a combination of such states, possibly of random intermittance.

The Bishop of Exeter's committee on the subject published some findings in a booklet entitled *Exorcism*. Otherwise the literature is patchy, ranging from the anti-occult works of the German pastor Kurt Koch (*Christian Counselling in Occultism* etc.), to more popular if facile books such as *Experiences of a Present-Day Occultist* by Donald Omand. Francoise Strachan's *Casting out Devils* gives a fairly well-balanced overview of the field. From the occult side there is Dion

Fortune's *Psychic Self-Defence*. David Blatty's novel *The Exorcist* dramatised many of the subjective and spiritual factors involved. There is a genre of films and paperback novels that over-emphasise the crude physical and sensational aspects.

EXTRA SENSORY PERCEPTION or ESP is a comparatively modern scientific term for the less understood powers of the mind, such as telepathy or clairvoyance. Dr. Rhine of Duke University has been a major figure in such work with the use of special cards with distinct markings of five different conventional signs.

Subjects in his experiments try to guess the identity of a card being looked at by another person and their degree of success is statistically analysed. Some people score consistently higher than would be expected from the law of averages if pure guesswork were involved. This suggests that they possess some degree of Extra Sensory Perception, sometimes called the *psi* factor. Other subjects seem able to guess accurately cards that are yet to come up (i.e. in the future).

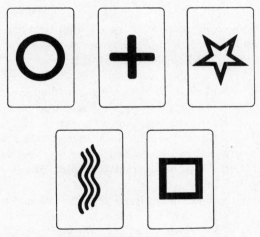

Cards used in ESP experiments

A general practical guide to the subject can be found in *How to Test and Develop your ESP* by Paul Huson.

FORTEANA is the name given to reported incidents that seem unexplainable by accepted scientific theories or indeed current common sense. The name comes from Charles Fort, an American journalist who collected and published several large volumes of such incidents, culled from press reports. They include rains of fish or frogs, teleportations, appearances of monsters, and so on.

GEOMANCY is a method of Divination (q.v.) in which a conventional set of 16 figures forms the staple pattern. The system is a western practice that is similar in principle to the Chinese I Ching (q.v.). A geomantic figure consists of four lines of pairs of dots or a single dot placed one above the other.

X X		X		X X	
X		X X		X X	
X X		X X		X	
X X		X X		X	

Geomantic figures

The traditional way to arrive at these figures is by random marks made in sand or earth (hence the term 'geo' – earth, 'mantic' – divination). Many modern consultants of the oracle feel that pencil marks on paper are equally valid.

A line of dots is made quickly without counting, in sixteen rows, and then each row is counted to see if it has an odd or even number. If an even number it is summed up by a pair of dots, if odd by a single dot. Thus from the sixteen lines, in accordance with certain rules of transposition, four geomantic figures, one above the other, are obtained. Other methods include selecting a number of pebbles at random from a dish, or throwing dice.

The method is given in full in Israel Regardie's useful little book on the subject *A Practical Guide to Geomantic Divination*.

As in all Divination one's attitude to the oracle is all important, and therefore the taking of some trouble to work with the original elements of sand or earth may well prove worthwhile rather than dashing off figures at random by idly making marks on paper.

Some trouble should be taken to cast an impression upon the mind that the results are important. Divinatory oracles tend to do as they are done by. It may not be easy to understand why this should be so but it is a wise rule of thumb by which to be guided.

GIFTS OF THE SPIRIT are first spoken of by the Apostle Paul in his letters to the Corinthians, who themselves became over-enthusiastic about the various strange gifts that attended Christian worship in those days. Paul himself spoke in strange tongues (1.Corinthians 14:18).

There is a movement within the church today, called Pentecostalism, that considers that such manifestations should still be a hallmark of Christian conversion. The powers of prophecy, speaking with tongues, healing and other charismatic gifts it considers to be gifts of the Holy Spirit.

Against this are those who ask if it is not rather just hysteria, sheer emotionalism or even the work of the Devil. In the latter category we tread on dangerous ground for it was on just such an occasion when Jesus was accused of working miracles by the power of the Devil that he turned on his accusers with the solemn warning that the "sin against the Holy Spirit" (that is, attributing its power blasphemously to the Devil), was the only sin that "could not be forgiven".

On the other hand there are no doubt many occasions when such gifts, or the desire for them, can get out of hand. Apart from the early attested experience of St. Paul, there have been many sects and groups within and without the church who have been distinctly cranky about it all.

The question becomes more confused when there are others who profess to do miraculous or supernormal things without the aid of religious conversion – as psychical or occult phenomena attending mediumship, or Uri Gella bending forks, allegedly by the power of thought.

There are undoubtedly powers of the human mind and body that are not fully understood or utilised. They can sometimes be developed by occult training but may also happen spontaneously as a result of a shake-up of the personality due to religious conversion. In the latter case it may seem to be, and indeed is in a sense, evidence of the power of God. For those who would enquire further into this complex subject, there is an excellent investigation of the matter called *Did You Receive the Spirit?* by Simon Tugwell, O.P.

HEALING can well manifest as a Gift of the Spirit, in which case it is called Spiritual Healing, sometimes Faith Healing, though the two may not be quite the same thing. The gift of healing by laying on of hands, as with other Gifts of the Spirit is, according to some, a gift which the church has neglected or lost, whilst others attempt to revive it.

There are famous religious centres, such as Lourdes, where many thousands go in search of divine cures, and though many are disappointed, and though there is a commercialism and hysteria about such places that are distressing, nonetheless there remains a small but significant percentage of people who are miraculously cured. The church authorities are, if anything, on the side of stringency in admitting any such miraculous occurrence, and they maintain careful medical checks on all alleged cures.

The Roman church does not have a monopoly in such practices, for there is the famous Anglican case of Dorothy Kerins who, as a child, was very near death through a complex of dreadful illnesses but miraculously recovered following a vision of Jesus and devoted her life to a mission of divine healing.

The best known healer outside the official churches was perhaps Harry Edwards who represents a movement in spiritualist and occult circles to heal by supra-physical means.

There are various other claims to the power of healing, some of which may be true but not admitted by medical science (cf. *Fringe medicine* by Brian Inglis) and others which may be verging on quackery. It is a particularly emotive and complex subject, but Dr. Leslie Weatherhead's *Psychology, Religion and Healing* can be recommended to anyone seriously approaching the subject.

The **HOLY GRAIL** has never been accurately defined, which perhaps adds to its awe and mystery. An important part of it is the 'Quest', and a quest for something that is not fully defined suggests a spiritual search in the soul of man rather than for a specific physical object. It is sometimes described in terms of a cup, or a dish, or a stone – in some versions as a precious stone, an emerald, that fell from Venus or from Lucifer's crown. Some say it is the vessel in which Joseph of Arimathea caught some drops of the blood of Christ, or the Cup of the Last Supper. Others think it to be of pagan origin, originally perhaps a cauldron of plenty, upon which Christian traditions have been overlaid. The Church itself has always tended to hold the Holy Grail tradition rather at arms length.

The Grail legends first appear in written literature between the years 1180 and 1220, and became part and parcel of the Arthurian legends.

The Apocryphal Gospel of Nicodemus, or the Acts of Pilate, is a source for much of the Holy Grail legend, with the story of Joseph of Arimathea, who sought Pontius Pilate's permission to take possession of the body of Christ, and to bury it in his own sepulchre. If one thinks of it, the role he played was of supreme importance to the subsequent events of the Resurrection story.

In the legends the Grail appears at a Grail Castle that is sought and found by the Grail Seeker. It is carried round in procession by a Grail Maiden, and as it proceeds all fall silent and each person's favourite food appears before them. It is perhaps significant that the Grail appears when all are seated at table.

It is important that the Grail Seeker ask three questions. If he fails to do so he is ejected from the place with great lamentation as having failed the test. Those who have been Grail winners have been variously named as Galahad, Percivale or Parsifal, and the good knight Sir Bors.

Joseph of Arimathea is also associated with Glastonbury, 'the holyest erthe in England' and tradition has it that he came to England, and struck his thorn staff into Wearyall Hill. There are indeed Grail traditions closely connected with Glastonbury as well as Arthurian lore.

The literature is vast but a sound introduction has been provided in *The Grail Seeker's Companion* by John Matthews and Marian Green. The Holy Grail and its quest can mean all things to all men but another useful guide to the possible varieties of approach is *At the Table of the Grail*, a collection of contributions by Grail seekers edited by John Matthews.

HYPNOSIS is a psychological technique whereby the subject is induced into a trance like state where the personal will goes into abeyance and the directions of the hypnotist are accepted at face value, whether true or false. The depth of trance may vary considerably and the ability to be hypnotised to a deep level varies from person to person.

In deep trance the subject can be anaesthetised and so the technique has been used to some extent in dentistry and to a lesser extent in surgery. However, it would appear that conventional forms of anaesthesia are considered by the dental and medical professions to be easier to administer and perhaps more reliable over the general range of patients.

The phenomenon has also been exploited by stage entertainers, where subjects are induced to perform amazing, amusing or ludicrous actions.

It can also be used in various forms of psychotherapy in order to overcome minor forms of addiction, to recover memory of past events, and even – by regression to times long past – to seek out memories of past lives.

In its original form it was associated with 18th and 19th century theories of 'animal magnetism' and 'odic force' and was known as Mesmerism, after the Viennese doctor Dr Anton Mesmer, who first exploited it.

I CHING is a Chinese system of philosophy, wisdom and divination. The symbols used are hexagrams, that is, six lines one above the other which may either be solid black lines or broken by a white space in the middle. Strictly speaking each hexagram is formed of two 'trigrams' but those who wish to follow through the detailed symbolism of this ancient Confucian wisdom should consult one of the excellent books now available on the subject; John Blofeld's *The Book of Change*, Diana Ffarington Hook's *The I Ching and You* or the original translation by Richard Wilhelm called *The I Ching or Book of Changes* which contains a foreword by Jung.

| 1. *Khien* | 2. *Air* | 3. *Sun* | 4. *Earth* |
| 5. *Water* | 6. *Moon* | 7. *Fire* | 8. *Khwan* |

I Ching tri-grams

The method of selecting the hexagram, which answer one's query, is by a complex selection of yarrow stalks or by tossing three coins. The latter method commends itself to busy Westerners who like to have everything, even oracular wisdom, available on tap with the absolute minimum of time and trouble. However, the more laborious and drawn-out yarrow stalk method may well be the better way in terms of conditioning consciousness to a properly receptive and enquiring attitude of mind.

The meanings of the hexagram are obtained by reference to cryptic paragraphs in the book. These are by no means easy to understand, which leads the sceptical to say that one reads one's own interpretation into them.

However, many who approach the oracle with respect and faith in its power and wisdom, testify to the help they have gained from it, though with warnings of the errors of becoming too credulous or degrading one's own will and judgement to that of the oracle, which has its own ways of knocking some sense into any foolish questioners.

KARMA is an Eastern doctrine that has been widely absorbed into Western occult thought and is largely concerned with explaining the reason why some people of obvious virtue suffer disastrous events in their lives whilst the wicked often flourish as the green bay tree. Allied to a belief in reincarnation it is the belief that the events and circumstances of the present are to a considerable extent determined by previous lives, and how one conducted oneself then. Similarly, virtuous action in this life will store up benefits in future lives, whilst wicked acts will inevitably draw upon themselves their just deserts in some future time.

In essence it is a belief in divine justice or cosmic balance, and the belief that good or evil deeds will, either by their own momentum, or through the ministrations of certain cosmic beings, or angels, have their just reward.

LEY LINES have become a highly popular topic in recent years. The concept rests upon the work of an amateur archaeologist, Alfred Watkins, who evolved a theory from his own fieldwork in the early years of this century. This was finally published in book form as *The Old Straight Track*. Watkins found that many ancient earthworks, many of them now the sites of churches, were built on straight lines, and he postulated that these were the markings of ancient trackways that formed trade routes and that in fact the straight Roman roads were often laid over them.

This theory was later elaborated by occult students because there were so many places of present and ancient worship along these lines.

There are two types of investigation; the psychic, which was able to 'feel' a different psychic atmosphere along these lines and particularly at the centres along it; and the scientific where researchers such as Professor Thom in *Megalithic Sites of Britain* and Gerald Hawkins in *Stonehenge Decoded* have produced evidence to suggest that the stone circles that mark many of these lines are in fact sophisticated astronomical computers and observatories. This suggests that our ancient forebears were not so ignorant nor primitive as we often assume.

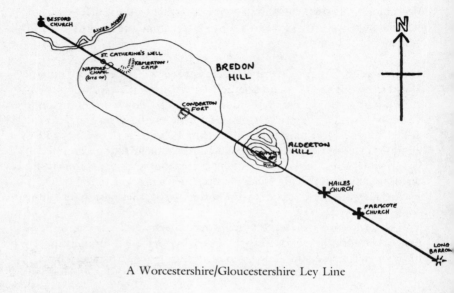

A Worcestershire/Gloucestershire Ley Line

There is some debate as to whether such lines are man-made or some sort of natural lines of geo-magnetism. There are traditions that the ancients had some secret source of motive power, perhaps as an aid to building their great earthworks and stone circles which involved considerable transportation and engineering problems. It may be a hint towards this that they seemed so anxious to be able to predict in advance eclipses of the moon. This no doubt had a religious significance but may well not be the whole story. If some form of subtle geo-magnetism was used then it would doubtless be subject to the moon's phases, as are the tides.

Another theory suggests that these lines could have been used psychically for navigation purposes, particularly at sea. The traditional wooden figurehead at a ship's prow may well be a vestige of a psychic maiden who guided the helmsman of ancient ships.

For intriguing extensions of the ley line theories there are John Michell's *The New View Over Atlantis* and other books. An excellent practical introduction to ley hunting is *The Ley Guide* by Paul Devereux and Ian Thomson.

LOST CONTINENTS are a kind of occult speculation into pre-history. The tradition is very strong of a lost continent somewhere in the Atlantic called Atlantis, and even for one before that, probably in the Pacific, called Lemuria.

Lewis Spence, a prolific occult historian writing between the wars, wrote much upon the subject in *The Problem of Atlantis, Atlantis in America, A History of Atlantis, The Problem of Lemuria, Will Europe Follow Atlantis?* etc. The famous clairvoyant Edgar Cayce also left much about Atlantis in his voluminous readings.

Like much in occultism, the legend has a strength of life far beyond what can justifiably be verified by the laws of scientific evidence. The legend is certainly an ancient one stemming from Plato, who in the *Critias* and *Timaeus* recorded Solon's study of the beliefs of the ancient Egyptian priests of his time.

There are perennial myths in the soul of man of a deluge or catastrophe – from Noah's flood to the destruction of Sodom and Gomorrah – and of a former Golden Age or Edenic state. Those who espouse the cause of Lost Continents regard such myths and legends as latent memories.

MAGIC is a greatly maligned and misunderstood term. In the general public mind it is closely associated with the production of apparently miraculous or marvellous events, by way of stage entertainment, where the modus operandi is the skilful sleight of hand or misdirection of attention by the illusionist.

It also has a more sinister reputation in the alleged use of secret psychic powers, often with rather sordid and blasphemous rites. This reputation has been developed by a particular genre of popular novels and the occasional sensational feature story in the gutter press.

In fact it is a term that needs to be rehabilitated from these misconceptions, for it originally meant a very high technical art of the human mind, namely the evocative use of the imagination by which spiritual insights could be gained of the world about us.

In this function it stands very close to the creation and appreciation of art of all kinds, and also of the traditional wisdom of the human race that is enshrined in myth and legend and popular story.

Its techniques are close to the techniques of analytical psychology,

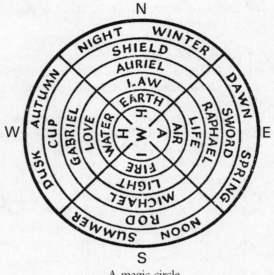

A magic circle

in that free fantasy, and meditation, and the visualisation of balancing (usually four-fold) patterns, play a large part in it. However, magic differs from psychotherapy in that its purpose is not confined to the curing of personal neurosis, but is intended to have a more general effect upon the inner levels of being that lie beyond the physical. These levels, or planes, are considered to be every bit as objective as the physical world, and can indeed have an effect upon the physical body or physical circumstances in certain ways.

There is a technical difference in magic between theurgy and thaumaturgy.

Theurgy is the spiritually motivated effort of helping to bring to physical expression the Will of God, or the Divine Plan. In this it is akin to prayer, particularly prayer of intercession, but seeks a more active role in mediating spiritual forces than the traditional mode of supplication or worship associated with prayer. Prayer is addressed to God, whereas magic is a means whereby, it is to be hoped, God's will is brought about by conscious contact with inner-world beings and forces.

Thaumaturgy is concerned with developing psychological powers in order to produce wonders, usually the teleportation of small objects or physical levitation of the subject or other feats of conscious control over the nervous system. Most occultists would question whether the end result is worth the prodigious effort in long and strenuous training but in the East such abilities are a firm part of the tradition of the discipline of the yogi, where, it should be said, the practitioner is expected to devote his whole life to it in monastic one-pointed intention and devotion.

Another more popular distinction is between White and Black Magic. This is a crude distinction between whether the motives involved are altruistic or selfish, aimed at the general good, or at working personal harm.

MANTRA (the plural form of Mantram) are phrases repeated either aloud or mentally in order to still the mind or to induce certain psychic or mystical states.

A familiar one in the East is the formula OM MANI PADME HUM, which, means, more or less, "the Jewel in the Heart of the Lotus" and refers, amongst other things, to the spiritual power behind the psychic centres, or chakras.

In the West there is the Jesus Prayer of the Orthodox Church "Lord Jesus Christ, have mercy upon me, a sinner." In some respects all popular prayers of church or childhood could be regarded as mantra if they are constantly repeated, from the Roman Catholic rosary to "Matthew, Mark, Luke & John, bless the bed that I lie on."

In a more psychological rather than religious context the technique formed a part of the popular movement for 'positive thinking' associated with Emile Coué, and the famous phrase "Every day and in every way I am getting better and better."

It is also possible to have mantra for specific purposes, and some oriental teachers particularly give a personal mantram to each of their students, for their exclusive use, which serves to link them to their own inner being and to the spirit of the teacher.

MASTERS, sometimes called by other titles, such as Mahatmas, Ascended Masters, or Inner Plane Adepti, are human beings who act as teachers and guides in occult matters. Whilst this function makes their role little different from that of a schoolmaster, or university professor, or master craftsman in charge of journeymen and apprentices, a somewhat unique feature is that a number of them are considered to be discarnate.

In this however they are no more unusual than the saints of the church, to whom the devout pray for intercession, although the role of a Master is more of a teaching and guiding one.

Occult teaching about them has become quite prominent over the past hundred years through the writings of H.P. Blavatsky, who openly claimed to be in touch with certain members of a trans-Himalyan brotherhood. This tradition has extended to identify also various Masters associated with other localities and variously considered to be incarnate or discarnate, with some difficulties arising over the use of terms, for there are subtle realms of the physical plane that some occultists define as 'inner' rather than physical, which are technically referred to as the etheric sub-planes.

However this kind of detail is not as important as the teaching which emanates from such sources, which is nowadays almost always through telepathic or clairvoyant or clairaudient means. It should be said that this can be variable in quality dependant upon the validity of the contact and the ability of the mediator who is providing the channel.

Together the Masters form a centre of consciousness that is usually known as the Hierarchy, or the Great White Lodge. It is commonly considered in occult circles that unless a group is contacted (consciously or unconsciously) by one or more of the Masters, it may well be able to function adequately as a discussion group or teaching circle, but cannot work with power. Some of the communications given through are indeed not intended to be so much discourses of knowledge as contacts of inner power, and such writings can indeed have quite a strong emotive or inspiring effect despite the sometimes less than remarkable informative content.

Also different occult groups have a different attitude toward promulgating their affiliation with the Masters. Some conceal it altogether, reserving such knowledge to their inner circle. Others make certain dark hints about 'secret chiefs', whilst others openly claim to give direct teachings from them, or to induce reverence and respect to certain figures. There is material for all tastes and it must be said that a certain amount of less than wise claims are made, ranging from the portentous to the sentimental. However, the existence of the Masters of the Wisdom is something that most experienced occultists take very seriously despite the occasional bad press.

Examples of books that discuss the role and existence of the Masters are *Initiation, Human & Solar* by Alice A. Bailey and the works of Mark L. and Elizabeth Clare Prophet. However the Masters have a strong permeating influence throughout a very wide range of modern esoteric literature.

MEDITATION means different things to different people and has various forms but basically it is a technique of concentrating the mind so that it circles about one key idea or object.

This is a help towards technical proficiency in occult work, which depends upon the ability to visualise clearly for relatively long periods of time. Its other purpose is to bore a shaft in conventional consciousness so that the shell of concrete ideation is pierced and the mind made consciously receptive to the intuitive faculty and what is generally termed the 'higher mind'. Conventional psychologists have only half the story in talking of a sub-conscious for there is a super-conscious too. In other terms, the way of meditation has been called a path from intellect to intuition.

Occult meditation might in fact be considered a training in intuitional awareness. A good general and practical guide is *Meditation: The Inner Way* by Naomi Humphrey, which sets out the basic techniques that are found in the many and varied systems.

NUMEROLOGY stems from the ancient teachings of Pythagoras.

There is, as with many branches of occult learning, a debased popular form of numerology. This simply substitutes numbers for letters in peoples' names and attempts to draw prophetic inferences from them. This stems from the Jewish mysticism of the Qabalah which studies the Old Testament in great detail, analysing words and letters for inner meanings. As, in Hebrew, letters are also used as figures, this leads naturally to analysing words numerically, and regarding those that add up to the same total to be connected in some way.

In the case of Proper Names in the Bible, there seems certainly a symbolism of this kind, and names are altered or invented accordingly. This is to be seen in the change of Abram's name to Abraham.

This complex coding also carried over to the Greek, and numerological correspondences can be found in the New Testament, particularly in the Book of Revelations. Those with a mind for it can construct or discover infinite ramifications of coding and symbolism.

The *Canon* by William Stirling is a classic title that gives a résumé of certain aspects of numerological symbolism in building; as do the more recent books by Nigel Pennick such as *The Ancient Science of Geomancy* and *The Mysteries of King's College Chapel*.

There is a lack of literature on the number symbolism of Pythagoras although there have been facsimile reprints of two notable eighteenth-century commentators, Thomas Taylor's *The Theoretic Arithmetic of the Pythagoreans* and Thomas Stanley's *Pythagoras*. However, this has been recently remedied by an excellent practical instruction book *Sacred Geometry: Philosophy and Practice*, by Robert Lawlor.

Less in the sphere of number, the archetypal insights available from a study of geometry, and more particularly its lesser known branch of 'Projective Geometry', have been ably laid out in *Encounters with the Infinite* by Keller-von Asten, and *Projective Geometry* by Olive Whicher. It is a legitimate branch of mathematics that has its own mathematical text books and literature and Keith Critchlow's *Order in Space* gives a useful range of archetypal insights in what is really a book on basic design. In this context Claude Bragdon's *Projective Ornament* ought also to be referred to.

PALMISTRY is one of those semi-sciences based on details of the human anatomy that, read analogically, aim to give indications of character and fortune.

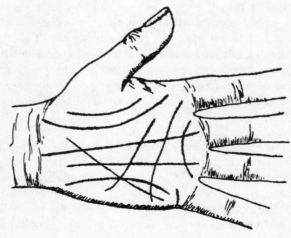

Lines of the hand

As with most of the so called 'occult arts' much depends upon the practitioner, and the occasional startling accuracy tends to counterbalance the large degree of shallow titilation and general superstition.

Apart from palmistry (the reading of lines on the hand) there are numerous other like disciplines from phrenology (the examination of bumps on the head) to physiognomy (the telling of character by facial characteristics).

PATH WORKING is a fairly modern expression that simply means use of the imagination to undertake an inner journey or to build up a specific symbolic scene. It is usually conducted in a group under the direction of an experienced leader.

It can be a powerful experience because the unified use of the imagination in this way has its effect upon each individual present. The mechanism of this is to be found in any theatre or cinema audience and indeed, in appropriate circumstances, with crowds of people anywhere.

It is also used by individuals as a technique of releasing unconscious memories or inhibitions in psychotherapy, where it is usually called 'free fantasy' or, if used in groups or with set formulae of specific symbols, 'initiated symbol projection'. In occult fraternities it has sometimes gone under more colourful terms such as 'scrying in the spirit vision'.

The term Path Working derives from the practice of using this imaginative technique in relation to the Paths on the Tree of Life, a popular esoteric symbol system.

Its published antecedents go back to the founder of the Jesuits, Ignatius of Loyola, whose *Spiritual Exercises* use the technique. In modern times a number of books have appeared giving scripts for workings of this nature. Examples are, using the Tree of Life, *The Shining Paths* by Dolores Ashcroft-Nowicki; using the signs of the Zodiac, *The Zodiac Explorer's Handbook* by Helene Hess; using traditional symbols *The Grail Seeker's Companion* by John Matthews and Marian Green, *The Western Way* by John and Caitlin Matthews, or *The UnderWorld Initiation* by R.J. Stewart; and using Tarot images *The Guide Meditation* by Ed Steinbrecher or *The Treasure House of Images* by Gareth Knight. *Highways of the Mind* by Dolores Ashcroft-Nowicki is a good recent book on the subject.

PLANES are different levels of consciousness or of perception, of which the physical is one. In occult cosmology there is generally held to be seven planes, although the detail of classification does vary. This is because inner space is as complex as outer space, and there are various ways in which it can be schematically described.

One of the most basic and simple classifications is as follows:

Spiritual
Intuitional
Mental
Emotional or Astral
Etheric/Physical

In this simple scheme the lower three are planes of Form, because they hold images, from mental pictures down to solid physical bodies and the etheric or electro-magnetic structure that holds them together organically. The two higher are called Formless, being abstract ideas, or direction or bias of the will, which are, it should be said, none the less powerful for that.

In occult training one learns to function consciously with organs of perception that function on the planes above the physical. On the lower levels this is done by working with mental pictures, on the higher levels it is done by working with abstract ideas.

The technique known as Path-Working is one instance of the former method of working. Meditation upon esoteric books of a high level of abstraction such as Dion Fortune's *Cosmic Doctrine* represent the latter method. The complete occultist will eventually be able to function on any of the planes at will.

The training is long, and like any discipline of learning can be tedious. However the training of inner organs of perception is similar to the training of the outer organs of perception which is what we all did in infancy, when it took us some years to appreciate and interpret the meaning of sights, sounds and the physical weight and texture of objects. Following that came the forming of social relationships, akin on the inner planes to the esoteric training involved in making contacts with inner beings and forces.

Different occult schools have their own precise formulation of the theory of the planes. One of the most comprehensive is Alice Bailey's *Treatise on Cosmic Fire* although a beginner might be better advised to start with something simpler such as one of the Theosophical Society publications by Annie Besant or C.W. Leadbeater, which however can be slightly misleading by reason of their attempt at simplicity. Again, as with the topic of Masters the doctrine of planes is taken for granted in a wide range of occult literature, so that the tyro tends to pick up the teaching without consciously noticing.

PSYCHICAL RESEARCH is the scientific investigation of phenomena that cannot be explained by current theories. We have dealt with E.S.P. (q.v.) and the term we now describe is traditionally more concerned with haunted houses, spiritualist mediums and phenomena that have no apparent physical causation.

The Society for Psychical Research was formed towards the latter end of the last century and still exists as a large repository of case-studies and investigations into these matters.

Whilst much valuable work has been done, to the occult student this line of research is severely limited by its own standards. This is all to the good as far as scientific integrity, reliability and responsibility are concerned, but if one is to investigate the non-physical by using only physical means then one works under a certain handicap. It is rather as if one tried to be an oceanographer by observing the sea from the land.

There are various kinds of psychical researcher, from the austere and rigorous laboratory scientist to the amateur and often feckless 'ghost hunter'.

Hauntings generally seem to divide into fairly specific types. There is, it would seem, a kind of 'photographic' principle whereby a scene from olden times (particularly if associated with strong emotion, such as violent death), is impressed on the locality and can be seen in certain circumstances. Another form, 'poltergeist' activity (literally, 'noisy spirit') seems to be caused by an excess of nervous energy at large and often emanates in some fashion from children at puberty or young women. The most common form, hardly to be detected by scientific instruments, is the atmosphere left behind by the departed or caused by their still being 'earth-bound' or linked somehow to the locality. Such psychic atmospheres can be uplifting and inspirational as well as at the other extreme, sad or dispiriting.

QABALAH is the theoretical basis for a large part of Western occultism. It is a Jewish system of thought, an important part of which is a diagram called the Tree of Life. Like other systems of symbolic correspondences, it can be used as a useful groundplan, or flow chart, of patterns of consciousness. It has a peculiar universality in that it can be applied to mystical as well as magical experience, and at various levels of mind. Thus it may be applied in a theological context as an outline of the attributes of God-head; or in a mythological context in comparing, one with another, various pagan pantheons of gods and legendary beings; at a magical level it shows the relationships of many and various symbols; at a psychological level it shows a ground-plan of the mind of man, particularly that part commonly known as the collective unconscious.

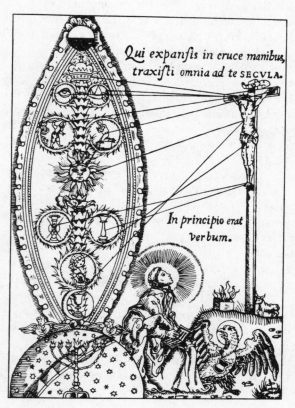

Sixteenth century Christian version of Qabalistic Tree of Life

One of the first and perhaps the best known book on the subject that makes relatively easy reading was Dion Fortune's *The Mystical Qabalah*, and Gareth Knight's *A Practical Guide to Qabalistic Symbolism* extends on from this. A few other useful introductory manuals have also been published in recent years, each from slightly differing points of view such as *The Ladder of Lights* by W.G. Gray; and *The Tree of Life* by Halevi.

The original Jewish Qabalah is based on two ancient books, *The Sepher Yetzirah* (or Book of Formation) and *The Zohar* (or Book of Splendour). These are not easy reading and in fact represent but a tiny part of the later Hebrew literature, which is vast and much of it untranslated.

From a standpoint of serious academic scholarship the works of Professor Gershom Scholem, *Major Trends in Jewish Mysticism* and *On the Kabbalah and its Symbolism*, are important works. The early little work, *The Kabbalah* by Christian Ginsburg, gives an excellent potted historical and philosophical outline.

REINCARNATION is a belief that we have lived on Earth before this life, and is quite widely accepted in occult circles. In Eastern religions, where it is also prevalent, it is associated with the law of Karma, wherein good or evil deeds performed in one life will have their result in conditions in a future life, and also the circumstances of this life have their origin in how we may have behaved in a past life.

Attempts at recovering memories of past lives have received some publicity, for the most part using techniques of hypnosis and recorded on tape by the hypnotherapist Arnall Bloxham.

RUNES are a set of symbolic signs that stem from the Northern lands, and originally carved on standing stones in Scandinavia, Scotland, Ireland and the Isle of Man, and there is also a strong Anglo-Saxon or Teutonic branch of the tradition. It has become popular in recent years as a means of making personal talismans or in divination. Popular works on the subject are Ralph Blum's *The Book of Runes* and *The Rune Workbook* by Tony Willis. (See figure page 90).

SPIRITUALISM is a movement that is generally conceded to have started in America in 1848 when the Fox sisters experienced strange knocking noises in their house, and responded to the ghostly manifestation by trying to set up communication.

The movement made tremendous progress in the 19th century and many homes formed their own family circle to experiment in trying to communicate with the departed. The most familiar means were

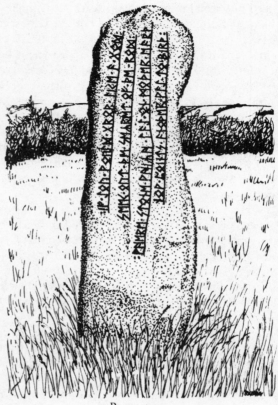

Rune stone

placing the hands upon a light table so that it could tilt and tap out
messages by a pre-arranged code. A slightly less laborious method
was the ouija board, a moving tablet which, when all present placed
their fingers upon it, could write messages or point to letters of the
alphabet placed in a circle.

There were also certain peculiarly gifted individuals who, by going
into trance, could cause physical phenomena to occur – the sight of
phantom forms and the movement of light objects. Direct voice
communication was also exploited, whereby the medium's vocal
chords were taken over, so to speak, by the communicating being.

Less dramatic but more common was a whole range of messages
received without deep trance, either clairvoyantly, clairaudiently or

by 'automatic writing.' All these techniques are methods whereby the conscious mind is made receptive to subconscious stimuli. In the case of genuine communication the theory is that a discarnate being can communicate in this way, by affecting the autonomic nervous system of the medium or the sitters. This might be a circle of people with their fingers on an upturned glass, or an individual holding a pencil on a sheet of blank paper with a completely receptive mind.

There is in all of this plenty of scope for unconscious self deception, or intended deception of others, and in the last analysis the validity of each case must be assessed by the quality of the messages received. Critics of the movement would say that these tend to be banal in the extreme, but on the other hand much of human communication is banal, and there are instances where material of quality has come through, even if no great works of literature. The amount of evidence is vast with books enough to fill a library. One centre of repute for sympathetically investigating this type of communication is the College of Psychic Studies, 16 Queensberry Place, London, and spiritualist organisations also exist, with many local branches and even churches, where practical evidence of such phenomena is freely presented. There is also a weekly newspaper devoted to the subject, entitled *Psychic News*.

TALISMANS, like many other items of an occult nature, are, in their more popular manifestion, part of the entertainment industry or of the jewelry trade. But behind the popular superstition of 'lucky charms' is a profound magical philosophy.

Even a lucky charm, mass-produced from cheap plastic or paste, may have a certain virtue if its wearer really believes in it. Like much else in occultism it cuts through religious and scientific boundaries in a disconcerting fashion. The scientist may see in the talisman an instance of auto-suggestion, the religious may deplore the idea of someone having more faith in a fetish than in God. Yet religious medallions are undoubtedly looked upon by their wearers in a talismanic way – as bearers of some kind of force or virtue. And every Catholic Christian altar contains relics of saints within or about it.

A true talisman, in the occult sense, contains a particular force. By the doctrine of correspondences, an object constructed of a certain material at a certain hour and bearing particular designs will act as a kind of lens for forces of a corresponding nature. Thus a talisman to attract love might be made of copper, engraved at an hour sacred to

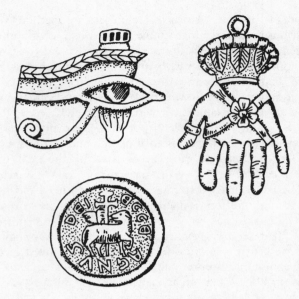

Christian and pagan talismans

Venus with a seven-fold figure or heptagram. Copper, Venus and the heptagram all bear symbolic correspondence to the quality of love.

In its highest use, as in magic of the Renaissance, talismans were used as a corrective to personality traits or imbalances. In many respects it is the work and ingenuity that goes into the making of a talisman that gives it its effectiveness and generally they work best for their maker.

Thus a true talisman is a custom-made artefact, made to a specific purpose and intention for a particular person, and not a mass-produced object. But a mass-produced object may well pick up strong beliefs held about it and thus be formed into an effective talisman by faith. Again there is something more than mere psychology to this because precious and semi-precious metals and crystals can be effective storage batteries of psychic force by virtue of their internal atomic structure.

TAROT cards are ancient playing cards and are full of deep and evocative symbolism. The four suits are Wands, Cups, Swords and Disks each with four Court Cards, a King, Queen, Knight and Page.

In addition to the four suits there are 22 trumps, numbered from 0 to XXI. The Zero Trump is the Fool. The others consist of the Magician or Juggler; the High Priestess, Female Pope or Pope Joan; the Empress; the Emperor; the Pope or Hierophant; the Chariot; the Lovers; Strength or Fortitude; the Hermit; the Wheel of Fortune; Justice; the Hanged Man; Death; Temperance; the Devil; the Lightning Struck Tower or House of God; the Star; the Moon; the Sun; the Last Trump and the World or Universe.

Marseilles Tarot cards

With this wealth of symbolism, which constitutes a complete symbolic model-universe, there is great scope for their use in divination. Serious students of the occult also use them for meditation or initiating waking dreams or visions. There has been a tremendous explosion of interest in the Tarot in recent years, with many packs available to suit all tastes and a considerable instructional literature.

Beginners would probably do best to start with a set of the fully pictorial Rider/Waite Tarot and the three books by Rachel Pollack give a comprehensive introduction to the system; alternatively *A*

Complete Guide to the Tarot by Eden Gray is something of a modern classic.

A detailed historical coverage is provided in Stuart Kaplan's *Encyclopaedia of Tarot* in two volumes, and his combined pack and book entitled *Tarot Classic* gives a comprehensive coverage on traditional lines of the old Marseilles tradition.

THEOSOPHY is the particular brand of occult teaching associated with a remarkable Russian woman, H.P. Blavatsky, who burst onto the occult scene in the Western world with two large and remarkable books, *Isis Unveiled* and then, more importantly *The Secret Doctrine* which since its publication in New York in 1888 has exerted a tremendous influence, often unrealised and unacknowledged, on much of modern occult thought.

The Theosophical Society was founded to expound and investigate these teachings, which included the promulgation of the existence of the Masters of the Wisdom. The headquarters of the movement subsequently moved to Adyar in India and with branches in most countries of the world. This was greatly helped by the efforts of two extremely energetic pioneers and publicists Annie Besant and C.W. Leadbeater.

The movement itself has had its ups and downs, as all human organisations do, but continues to maintain an international presence, even where some branches have split off from the parent body. The formal organisation apart, the teachings have exerted a widespread influence and have been the spring board for other teachers of considerable note, who have formed schools or movements of their own, such as Rudolf Steiner or Alice A. Bailey.

A considerable literature exists which, for those able to visit London, is perhaps best examined either at the Theosophical Bookshop in Bury Place, or at the headquarters at 50 Gloucester Place, where meetings and lectures are also given.

UFO's are not necessarily of the occult though they do tend to get lumped in with it, particularly as many contacts are claimed to have been made through occult means, such as telepathy. The literature is vast and ranges from the serious attempts at systematic recording of sightings to lunatic accounts by imaginative cranks. This is a reflection of how things tend to be in the occult field. *UFOs 1947–1987* edited by Hilary Evans gives a serious and complete enquiry into this many sided subject.

WITCHCRAFT has undergone a revival in recent years, partly through the efforts of Gerald Gardner and his books *Witchcraft Today* and *The Meaning of Witchcraft*, although there are branches of the tradition which would claim to be more ancient and authentic. The general tone has not been improved by publicity, and individuals claiming high-sounding titles for themselves.

The movement is a form of nature mysticism or Neo-Paganism, but the term witchcraft seemed to appeal more to the imagination if not always for the best of reasons.

A 17th century perception of witchcraft

Most witches we have met have been sincere, religious-minded people who could not accept the institutionalised Christianity of our times and had turned to some kind of nature-worship as a means of religious self-expression.

Books worth studying for a general groundwork of the Old Religion include *The Lost Gods of England* by Brian Branston and the relevant works of Dr. Margaret Murray, *The Witch Cult in Western Europe*, *The God of the Witches* and *The Divine King in England*. Robert Grave's *The White Goddess*, contains much basic material and is highly thought of by many students of the subject. Doreen Valiente's *An*

ABC of Witchcraft is a useful vade mecum on the subject, whilst Charles Leland's *Aradia, The Gospel of the Witches*, hitherto a rare nineteenth-century book, has been recently reprinted and is an important source work.

YOGA means 'union' and is an oriental discipline for the integration of the inner powers of the soul and body. It has various aspects, for instance *raja yoga* pertains to the mind, *bhakti yoga* to the emotions and *hatha yoga* to the body. The latter, simplified, has found a vogue in the West for its physical exercises although there is very much more to the subject than callisthenics.

In the complete system of *hatha yoga* the physical postures are accompanied by complex breathing and visualising techniques which direct forces through the channels of the subtle body – whose link with the physical body is via the endocrine glands. This is very powerful and can be dangerous to perform without close personal supervision by a yoga master. Eventually it can lead to quite incredible feats of bodily control.

The more complex postures are not easy for a Western body to adapt to, and those who take up the advanced study of yoga really need to have a burning vocation for it and to be prepared to go to the East, or at least to live a relatively enclosed or highly disciplined life close to a yogin, if one can be found in the West.

The West has its own techniques which are more suitable to our physique and temperament.

The most popular books about yoga probably remain the works of Yogi Ramacharaka – *Raja Yoga, Gnani Yoga, Hatha Yoga, Yoga Philosophy* and *Oriental Occultism* etc, – who, under his real name of William Walker Atkinson, was quite capable of writing works on practical Western occultism such as *The Secret of Mental Magic*.

PART THREE
First Steps on the Occult Way

GETTING TO KNOW YOURSELF

The study of the occult is essentially a practical one. Therefore it is often called the Path, or the Way. And even if your studies seem to be no more than book learning in the first instance, this still is a practical step along the Occult Path or Way, which is a way of self knowledge.

And self knowledge means a knowledge of your own subjective world – which has more influence upon the objective world in which you find yourself than you might at first think. All knowledge of the world about you comes to you through your physical senses, but is also processed by your inner attitudes and expectations and prior assumptions. Therefore, however little control you may seem to have on the events going on about you, they are certainly perceived by you through tinted spectacles.

We say of one who is an incurable optimist that they are "looking at the world through rose-tinted glasses" – implying that they are not seeing things as they 'really' are. However, we all have our own tinted, or even distorting lenses through which we view the world, and one of the first tasks is to 'cleanse the doors of perception.'

This is why from the earliest records of occult tradition, it is found that 'Know thyself' is the first injunction to every seeker of hidden, or occult, truth. It was engraved at the portal of the world famous oracle of Delphi in ancient Greece. And it remains as true today as it was then.

How do we get to know ourselves? It is not quite so easy a task as might at first appear. If we find it difficult to see the outer world as it really is, it is even more difficult to weigh up the inner thoughts and motivations of our friends, family and acquaintances, and next to impossible to look at ourselves accurately and know what really makes us tick. However, it is this difficult task that is attempted by anyone who seriously takes up the study of the occult.

It is true that there is a very great deal of superstitious nonsense that is bandied about in the name of occultism by people whose grasp of the realities of the outer world and their own condition of soul could hardly be further from the truth. Occultism, by its concentration upon the subjective side of life, (at any rate in the early stages), attracts its share of the immature, the inadequate, and the unbalanced, who are seeking some kind of escape from the outer world. However, this phenomenon of a 'lunatic fringe' occurs in most areas of study where the subjective plays an important role – such as the arts, or even politics.

Thus the first two traditional virtues of any seeker after occult truth are Discretion and Discrimination. One has to develop the ability to discern the wheat from the chaff. And also not be put off by outward appearances, nor on the other hand fooled by them. We have used the phrase 'seeker after occult truth' – and that really sums up this stage of the Path, which is that of the Seeker.

THE SEEKER AND THE QUEST
The search for occult truth tends to fall into a series of identifiable stages. The average man or woman of the world may well have no interest in such matters but be quite content with the relationships and situations in which they find themselves in the physical world. A world that is generally bounded by family relationships, business or career ambitions, and the pleasurable pursuit of leisure activities, all of which may be pursued in the context of conventional religious belief and practice (or lack of it) to a greater or lesser extent.

The Seeker is someone to whom all of this, laudable as it well may be, and the norm of general civilised behaviour, becomes inadequate. Something somehow is missing. This can come like a bolt from the blue, or be a generally increasing awareness, that may well come on in later life.

This can be a very miserable period for such a person, as they may well not realise what is happening, and may feel guilty that – perhaps in the midst of plenty, and a loving family – they are discontented. However, it is a very natural process of the beginning of self knowledge in the occult sense. The discontent, (sometimes it is called the 'divine discontent'), comes from the higher unconscious levels of their being, which are calling for a measure of conscious recognition.

This feeling can also come to those quite young, and can then be even more of a problem, as it can divert them from the very necessary business of preparing themselves by education and training for a responsible and fulfilling role in material life, and this gives the phenomenon of the 'drop-out', whose pursuit of vague ideals overcome all thoughts of immediate and future practicalities.

However, at whatever stage in life it comes, it is in essence no pursuit of vague ideals, even though to an unsympathetic observer it might well appear to be such. There is nothing wrong with ideals, the whole of civilised existence is built upon the pursuit of them, however far the reality may often fall short. They are of necessity vague, however, to some extent until the Seeker has formulated exactly what he or she is looking for.

Something of this dilemma is mirrored in the legends of the Quest of the Holy Grail. This is a search on the part of one of the knights of the Round Table of King Arthur, who is thus, by definition a Seeker. However, nobody seems to know what the Holy Grail is, or even what it looks like. In some tales it is in the form of a cup, in others it is a stone, others see it as a dish, to name but a few of the versions. Yet it is none the less real for all that, and has a profound effect upon those who seek it, whether or not they find it, and on the whole realm in general.

So anyone in the position of the Seeker is seeking for something they know not how to define, or even if it exists. Not unnaturally this can cause some concern, incomprehension, and even irritation and hostility from family and friends.

Some may find a remedy of sorts in greater involvement in church or charitable activities. This can be a step in the right direction, for the higher consciousness that is trying to make itself felt is more concerned with expression in a wider field of service than is generally to be found in the well motivated but essentially self centred concerns of the normal man or woman of the world.

However, there is still likely to be a sense of unfulfilment because the type of inner awareness or experience that is to be found in many religious institutions goes nowhere near fulfilling the hunger of soul that can experienced by the Seeker. In the more conventional forms of religious observance indeed, such awareness or experience may be almost entirely lacking, being what one broad churchman once defined, with some self-satisfaction, as "morality tinged with emotion".

Thus the Seeker will usually need to seek beyond the confines of established religious thinking, which is a pity in one way, because there is profound truth and experience of a spiritual nature to be found there, but all too often hidden under a very heavy layer of stale custom and convention.

This means that a lot of books need to be read, or at least looked at, because every single Seeker is different, and the paths to inner wisdom and self knowledge are very diverse. So which way is the right one is the question that every Seeker has to ask, and find the answer for. This may well mean a few false starts, but no time or experience is ever wasted in the long run. It is to be hoped that this book, with its general notes on a variety of aspects of occultism, together with suggested introductory reading, will help a few Seekers to find their true way with a little more facility.

However, until that way is found, some general practical guidance can be provided, for although all the individual paths are different, and some are broad ways paved by long established Societies, and others more narrow and less trodden paths, they all cover broadly the same ground – which is the quest of the higher consciousness, and its expression in the world. To this end, we give the following practical notes, which should stand any genuine Seeker in good stead, and enable the initial steps of the Path to be trod.

TYPES OF MEDITATION
Most, if not all, occult progress depends upon the practice of meditation. There are in fact a number of forms of meditation, but in general it simply means the practice of turning the focus of conscious attention inwards instead of outwards, for a time.

In its most rigorous form it may be the practice of thinking about 'nothing' for a period of ten or twenty minutes. This is no easy feat, and it is more rewarding for most of us to think about 'something' – which can indeed be equally productive. Various schools or teachers will advocate different subjects upon which to concentrate in this way. With some it will be a phrase, repeated over and over again. This is sometimes called a mantram, and in the East, where it has a strong following, the phrase will be especially selected and given to the individual student according to his inner needs as discerned by his teacher. Those without a teacher can choose an ideal or motto that appeals to them, and which reflects their aspirations. This phrase can be changed from time to time as each gets worked out, so to speak. An example might be "Per Ardua ad Astra" – "through glory to the stars".

A famous example is the Jesus prayer of the Orthodox church, or indeed the Ave Maria of Roman Catholic observance. In the East there are also well known universal mantra such as Om Mani Padme Hum – or simply the sacred word Om or AUM – which starts at the back of the throat and is articulated gradually more forward until the M sound made with the lips. This universal mantram is generally translated as meaning "the jewel in the heart of the lotus". In symbolic terms this is what the Seeker is seeking. It is a form of the Holy Grail. The jewel is the higher consciousness that lies at the heart of the flower of the personality. Om or Aum itself, is generally untranslatable, but signifies by its very articulation, the divine creative process, from the depths of the throat (the higher creative centre) to the humming expression of the lips in the outer world.

Therefore, in these simple actions the whole of the occult Path is contained in essence. However, in the last analysis the Path has to be expressed or trodden out in daily life – sitting for a few minutes each day meditating in seclusion is a start, and a beneficial practice for a long time to come, but is not the whole story.

Other forms of meditation may be more discursive. That is a phrase may be meditated upon with the expectation of receiving 'realis-ations'. This is a way that teaching may be brought through to the conscious mind from the deeper levels of one's being. In a sense it is a controlled form of dreaming.

Taken to its ultimate level such meditation can spawn forth whole books. It should be said that these may be of varying merit. We can all tap these levels within ourselves but it is only the few that are able to do so to the extent and quality of being the authors of inspired communications that are worthy of being disseminated to the world at large. This is an exact parallel of the fact that all or most of us can write poetry or tell stories, which may well be appreciated by our friends and serve as a fulfilling channel of creative effort for ourselves, but not all of us are destined to be great writers.

However some of the key books of occult tradition were received by regular meditation in this time honoured fashion.

At a less verbal and mentally conceptual level there is meditation in picture images. This is a very powerful and rewarding mode of work, although also one where there is some risk of 'glamour' and self-deception.

By glamour we mean too literal an interpretation of some of the images that may come to mind. If angelic forms appear in the imagination it is not necessarily the fact that the recipient is in direct conscious contact with the highest heavens. However, as with the more mental forms of meditation, and indeed all occultism in general, it is common sense and a healthily maintained sense of proportion, that must rule the day. It is important to believe implicitly in what one subjectively experiences at the time, otherwise the visions will wither, but it is even more important to assess their true value in the cold light of day. It is for this reason that a teacher, or spiritual director, is recommended by most schools of thought. As in all subjects, self tuition is possible, but general guidance by an experienced teacher can save some embarrassing excursions into self deception.

SYMBOLIC MAPS AND IMAGES
The visual images that can be used for meditation are many and various. They range from static simple images, such as a gold cross with a rose in the centre, to very complex ones such as the Tree of Life. Indeed, comprehensive images such as the Tree of Life contain a wealth of symbolism that can be worked upon in detail.

There are, for instance, ten spheres on the Tree of Life, any one of which contains a great deal of images in itself. Enough to provide meditation material for weeks. Much the same could be said for diagrams, or sequences of diagrams, to be found in spiritual alchemy. The secret of penetrating the mysteries that these contain is to imagine them before you, as pictures, not to try to work out their meaning by mental speculation. This same criterion applies to more familiar systems of occult symbols, such as Tarot cards or the hexagrams of the I Ching, to say nothing of the much abused and vulgarised signs of the Zodiac.

As well as picturing such images in a static form before you, it is possible to make them the starting point of a personal experience, by walking into them or through them, in the imagination. When applied to the Tree of Life, this technique is often applied to walking the paths that join one sphere to another – hence the term 'path working', which has come to be applied to any such excursion even when not ostensibly connected with the paths of the Tree of Life. In the system of the Hermetic Order of the Golden Dawn it used to be called 'scrying in the spirit vision' but its antecedents go back a very long way indeed. The founder of the Jesuits, Ignatius of Loyola, elaborated his series of Spiritual Exercises by just such visionary processes applied to scenes from the Bible. We can be assured, from hints dropped in various ancient texts, that this method was very much the modus operandi of the ancient Mysteries, whether of the classical world or ancient Egypt. It is also how myths and legends were developed by bardic story tellers and later ballad singers. And the same basic techniques are to be found from the esoteric schools of the Orient to the religious practices of the American Indians or Australian aborigines.

However, some sort of system needs to be worked to if one is not to be a mere 'day tripper' of the inner worlds, seeking and getting only a disorganised range of unrelated experience. There can indeed be a certain educative element in such an approach but generally speaking some kind of map is an advantage when venturing into strange lands.

There are of course different maps, of which the Tree of Life is one, which is particularly well known in Western occult circles. However, generally speaking all maps of the inner world are based on the inner structure of the human being. We are considerably more than the mobile biological systems that constitute our physical bodies. Behind this physical body, holding it together in a kind of electro-magnetic matrix, is the etheric body. This is sometimes discerned as the aura, under certain conditions, and is the vehicle of consciousness for those people who have had 'after death' experiences. Such experiences have become more frequently reported in the light of recent advances in medical techniques of resuscitation after heart attacks. The person generally finds himself floating free from the physical body, often at ceiling height, viewing all the attempts of the medical team at revival.

However, we do not seek to teach how to attain such experiences at will. This is technically known as etheric projection, (often mis-called astral projection), and is not a normal or natural condition to be sought after. In life the etheric body is an integral part of the physical body and their separation in full consciousness belongs only to very advanced techniques of yoga, or as the result of physical trauma. There are only a very few individuals to whom it may come naturally or in the early stages of the occult Path.

The etheric double is not an amorphous cloud. Like the physical body it has its specialised organs, generally known as chakras, or psychic centres, which are whirling vortices of psychic energy. The aim of practical occult development is to make changes in the centre of consciousness, which will in fact cause changes in the etheric vehicle and indeed ultimately in the subtler aspects of the physical vehicle too. This is done by techniques of imaginative visualisation, in meditation.

The use of the creative imagination is what is called the astral level of consciousness in occult work, and is also the level of psychic perception. In the training of a yogi work at the astral level is allied to work at the etheric level in a series of complex breathing exercises, which are allied to detailed visualisations centred on various parts of the body, and with the taking up of specific physical postures, often very difficult for a Westerner to attain. Only in rare cases is it advisable for a Western person, living the kind of life that goes with Western civilisation, to attempt to use full blown Eastern methods of development such as this. There may be modified versions watered down so as to be little more than physical fitness and mental relaxation exercises, which can indeed be beneficial at their elementary level, and which are frequently taught at college evening classes these days. However, the complete yogic method is designed for Eastern souls and bodies, and in conditions of life that are very different too. So unless one can live the life of a hermit and devote most of one's waking hours to it, these techniques are best left alone by most Westerners. What is likely to happen is a heightened psychic sensitivity that cannot cope with the hurly burly and cruder psychic vibrations of Western life, leading to physical debility and nervous exhaustion.

DEVELOPING THE PSYCHIC CENTRES

The Western technique is quite safe and has been practised over centuries. It works directly upon the astral or imaginative levels, without linking in to the etheric body by special breathing techniques or postures. The normal position to take up is of being seated, with spine straight, the thighs parallel with the floor, the hands and fore-arms resting upon them, and the feet squarely placed on the ground (or on a foot-stool if this makes the posture better in relation to the height of the seat of the chair). The ideal to aim for is relaxed poise.

The only breathing technique that is necessary is perhaps a few fairly deep regular breaths to begin with to help initial relaxation. Some people like to do this to a count of four, and to maintain this rhythm throughout their meditation work, but it is not essential and is largely a matter of personal preference and the type of meditation one may be undertaking. The main thing is not to "over-breathe" – leading to over-oxygenation.

Of the various centres in the human organism by far the most important for our immediate purpose are three. That is, a point above the head; the heart; and a point just below the feet. It may seem strange that two of these centres are outside of the physical body but as has been said above, we are not all physical, and our aura extends a considerable way beyond.

By far the most important of these three is the point above the head. It represents our own spark of divine consciousness, our own real self. It may be called various names by different schools of occult thought but the mental labels we choose to put upon things are not all that important.

We suggest you try the following sequence.

When you have composed yourself in meditation concentrate your thought about six inches above your head and imagine a brilliant white light there. You may well be surprised at the ease with which this supposedly subjective image builds up and feels to be actually there. When you are conscious of it being well and truly there try seeing a ray of this white light proceeding from it, forwards and downwards, so that it forms a large arc before your body, and comes in again at the point about six inches beneath your feet. Be aware of it then ascending behind your back to join up again with the centre of brilliant light from whence it started.

Having done that satisfactorily, see and feel the circle revolve upon its axis so that you are standing inside a sphere traced out by this line of light.

Now feel a line of light from this point above your head proceeding forward at an angle inside the sphere of light you have made, until it reaches the level of your heart. See it, a few inches inside the shell of the sphere of light, then turn toward your heart and come inwards to the centre of your heart. You may well feel a warm glow when this occurs.

Having got this far, now feel radiations going from your heart to fill the whole sphere about you with golden light. You may also see a symbolic picture form within your heart. It could be a picture of a revered master or saint, it could be a dove, or a cross, or a questing knight, or a radiating sun. In essence it represents your own spiritual self channeling through the heart centre, which is the centre of expression for your own higher consciousness.

You may conclude by seeing a further line of light go from the angular point before your heart, down toward the centre beneath your feet. As you do this feel the floor glow beneath your feet with the light of the spirit, and be aware that this is the light to light your path through life.

Having done all this you can gradually let the light fade inside the sphere, see and feel the sphere contract into a circle of light as it was in the beginning, and then running backwards from the top of your head, retract itself into itself all round the circle until it returns to being a single radiating point above your head.

Then bring your consciousness back to your physical surroundings, gently but firmly.

THE PATH TO FURTHER PROGRESS
This exercise should serve to start you on the right path and to give a certain amount of experience as to some of the possibilities of meditation. The exercise is capable of very considerable development and in various different ways, although it would not serve any real purpose to elaborate such details here. Other books of my own give due means of development in different ways. *A Practical Guide to Qabalistic Symbolism* gives a very full treatment of the symbolism of the Tree of Life, which is the basic ground plan of occultism through Western methods. *Experience of the Inner Worlds* gives a sequence starting from the Sphere of Light which gives a Christian oriented path of inner awareness. *The Rose Cross and the Goddess* shows how a four-fold system based on the traditional four elements, and the feminine principle, can be developed. *The Treasure House of Images* gives practical work based upon the Tarot, and *The Secret Tradition in Arthurian Legend* spells out in some detail a way of progress using legendary Arthurian and Holy Grail themes.

There are of course other methods provided by other teachers, many of whose works are mentioned in earlier pages of this book.

It may seem that all this is an embarrassment of riches. However until a particular path is found which will suit the Seeker for life, or at any rate for a fair amount of progress, the basic outline given above will give something practical to do that will prove of worth as a preliminary to almost any system of further development.

It can indeed provide a basis of profound occult experience in its own right if persisted in, bringing about an ever more conscious and purposeful indwelling of the immortal spirit in the daily life. It can be utilised in any circumstances of daily life. The spirit is always with you whether you realise it or not, and in moments of stress, or even boredom on a public transport system, the point of light above the head can be invoked, the sphere of light built, and the heart centre activated.

This does not mean that we recommend the practice of opening oneself to psychic impressions in a random and undisciplined way. This can play havoc with the sensibilities and emotional balance of anyone who is naturally sensitive to psychic atmospheres. But the activation of the head and heart centres in the way we have described, renders one positive rather than negative to the psychic environment on the lower levels. Thus it can even be a protection in hostile or unsympathetic psychic environments.

Furthermore, this should not take the place of set daily meditation, which gives best results if conducted in one particular place at a regular time. But occultism is nothing if it cannot be related to everyday life and circumstance. The benefit of regular meditations in a place set apart is that it teaches, and takes advantage of, two fundamental occult laws. One is that places can take on a particular vibration if persistently worked in with the forces of higher consciousness. The other is that rhythm has a fundamental role in all life, and regularity of occult work is another form of rhythmic expression that can pay dividends if intelligently utilised.

And above all, success in occultism, by whatever standard one measures it, is dependent upon right motive. The activation of the divine spark above the head, and its expression through the heart and beneath the feet, is a way to discover and live out that right motivation.

From this can follow the pursuit of any occult vocation, be it in the field of teaching, or of counselling, or of healing. Whatever the general public opinion of the occult may be, misguided through popular journalism or sensational cheap novels, its pursuit is a long and arduous one and its underlying motive one of service, and often in ways that are barely understood by the workaday world. Even, in some times and climes, barely tolerated.

However, it is a high calling, that leads to high adventure, and that calls for high standards. No-one who has a sense of vocation for it would settle for anything less!